The
Senate
Establishment

By
JOSEPH S. CLARK and Other Senators

Foreword by
JAMES MacGREGOR BURNS

American Century Series
HILL AND WANG • NEW YORK

FIRST EDITION AUGUST 1963
SECOND PRINTING OCTOBER 1963
THIRD PRINTING NOVEMBER 1963
FOURTH PRINTING APRIL 1964
FIFTH PRINTING APRIL 1965
SIXTH PRINTING MAY 1966

Manufactured in the United States of America

Foreword by James MacGregor Burns

SOMETHING stirs in the hearts of men when someone challenges authority and tradition—when a young churchman nails his theses to a church door, or when an author accuses the military of injustice against a Jew, or even when a boy asks for a second bowl of porridge. The stir may be quiet, hardly noticed; the walls of the establishment may feel no tremor; the establishmentarians may not deign to reply. But the word has been said, the deed performed, and nothing is ever again quite the same. Only in later years, as historians set their surveyors' stones, do people realize that the word or deed was the beginning of an end.

Does it seem far-fetched to compare the United States Senate to a great religious establishment, an American Senator to a Zola? Not to those who see the far-reaching ramifications of Senate power. For the Upper Chamber is not a lonely, beleaguered citadel, as some of its admirers assert. It is a visible apex of a pervasive system of power, which I have described elsewhere as a Congressional party system. The Senate part of this system is rooted in one-party states in the North and South. It is based in the Senators' six-year tenure, which guarantees that on the average half the Senators have been elected in "off" years between Presidential elections. It is strengthened by ancient Senate techniques for fortifying minority (i.e., conservative) power—discrimination against liberals in the selection of important committee memberships and chairmanships, parliamentary rules that block and enervate the majority, and, of course, the power to filibuster.

Presiding over this structure of power is the bipartisan coalition that Senator Clark attacked in his speech against the establishment. This is the coalition of the Democratic Congressional party and the Republican Congressional party—the parties of Howard Smith, Joe Martin, Robert Taft, Harry Byrd. This coalition embraces the power of the great fiscal committees—Finance and Appropriations in the Senate, Ways and Means and Appropriations in the House—and Rules in the House, which commands major avenues to the "Big Four." For a few months every Presidential election year the coalition is suspended, as Congressional leaders give at least lip-service support to their Presidential party candidates. But for three and one-half years out of four, the Congressional parties combine in a loose alliance to thwart the legislative program of a liberal Republican or liberal Democratic President.

Senator Clark's speech is of historical significance because it aims squarely at this century-old coalition as it operates quietly in the Senate. He has moved the power process out of dim and musty committee and caucus rooms into the spotlight of the Senate floor. I will not expand on this brilliant performance because the address speaks for itself. But I must note other qualities of the speech that may escape the reader who is looking only for the drama of the confrontation.

For one thing, this speech, along with the notable contributions of Senator Douglas and other Senators, abounds in *facts.* It is not a windy attack on some obscure and distant conspiracy; it is filled with "inside information," if you will—with names, votes, line-ups. Hence it is a superb case study in the exact operations of one of the chief instruments of Congressional party power—control over committee appointments.

Then, too, this speech shows the Senate off at its best. Is it paradoxical that an attack on Senate ways should evoke some of the best speeches, and exchanges on the floor, that the Senate has seen in recent years? Perhaps not, because the Senate, like other institutions under fire, may show its mettle in the face of opposition. In any event, Senator Mike Mansfield's answers to

Clark are a notable defense of Senate ways; it is a pity, though, that some genuine leader of the establishment did not deign to pick up Clark's gauntlet.

Finally, the discussions following the speeches continually pique our curiosity and make us want more information. Was Senator Javits really as philosophical as he appeared about being jettisoned by the Congressional Republican leadership and dumped from the Appropriations Committee? (His later remarks suggest that he was not.) What about the moderate Democrats who seem to favor President Kennedy's program but who vote to support coalition arrangements that will block that program? Are they ignorant of the relations of ends and means? Or is this politically the best behavior for them, enabling them to take liberal positions rhetorically without needing to take liberal action on policy? The fact that New York, the "mother of Presidents," has had only five men on the Senate Appropriations committee from the beginning—does not this little fact illuminate the contrasting methods of recruitment in the Congressional and Presidential parties? And what insight do we gain into the Presidency—did President Kennedy really show "no interest" in Senator Clark's proposal to liberalize the Senate Finance Committee? That is what Senator Mansfield says, and he is an honest man. Was the President *really* not interested? This seems doubtful. Was he simply following a "correct" hands-off procedure even in his *private* dealings with the Senate majority leader? If so, to whom, if anyone, did he indicate interest in the committee that could kill or cripple his legislative proposals? Many other questions will occur to the perceptive reader.

And what next? This book concludes with a magnificent speech by Senator Douglas, who has been observing and pondering Senate ways for a decade and a half. His colleague from Pennsylvania, Senator Douglas told the Senate, had helped to "ring a firebell in the night." Was it a firebell? The Senate establishment seemed hardly to move; at times only three Senators were listening to Clark on the floor. Perhaps the people were listening; it was hard to tell. The publication of this volume may hasten the day when people will not only listen but will act—and act not only to strengthen the Senate as a representative and democratic institution, but to modernize our whole deadlocked system of government. If they do, historians may decree that the beginning of the end really did begin that February day when Senator Clark rose on the Senate floor to challenge the bipartisan conservative coalition that had become an establishment.

Preface by Senator Joseph S. Clark

IN 1960 a new generation came to political power in the United States. John F. Kennedy made it a keystone of his campaign for the Presidency that it was time for a change of command not only in policies, programs, and personalities but in years. Had Vice-President Nixon been elected, much would have been different, but one important thing would have been the same: the old generation would have given way to the new. Both Kennedy and Nixon are twentieth-century men, and the campaigns they waged, and the platforms on which they ran, look to the future and not to the past. Kennedy said he would get the country moving again; Nixon said he would build on the foundation laid by Eisenhower; both committed themselves to a change in the status quo.

For the Supreme Court, time has done what Franklin Roosevelt failed to do—bring the Court into the twentieth century. Today, the nine old men are not only younger in years, but—far more important—they are younger in outlook. They are men of our time, who understand the problems of our time. Indeed, in some instances—notably civil rights—they have exerted a praiseworthy leadership which has left the other branches of government, and many people in our society, behind. Certainly those changes which are most persistently pressed with regard to the powers of the Supreme Court are not intended to speed up the pace of the Court's progress—far from it—but rather to disinherit us of the democratic legacy which the Court has in recent years been bequeathing.

It is in the third branch of government, the legislative branch, where political lag remains triumphant, and where the twentieth-century men are not in charge. Though the Senate has been shaken by wars, deaths, the electorate, and other calamities, those in it dedicated to the preservation of the status quo in economic and property rights and to the past in human rights—that bipartisan conservative coalition which I have called the "Senate establishment"—have still not given way to the new generation.

It is in fact more than a generation since the last successful attack was made on the Senate establishment. In 1913, the Democrats, having captured control of the Senate for the first time in sixteen years, revolted against the party leadership, and proceeded to emasculate the old seniority system, democratize the Senate's rules and procedures, wrest committee domination from the conservative coalition, and enact the progressive legislation of President Wilson's New Freedom.

The time has come to do it again. The national interest requires it. The modern world requires it.

But it may well be asked: why, in a Senate made up of sixty-seven Senators of the President's own Democratic party, with thirty-three Senators of the minority Republican party, should it be necessary to do this. And it may further be asked why the critical battles for control of the Senate took place as intraparty matters—in the Democratic Steering Committee, in the Republican and Democratic Conferences (of which the public has probably never heard)? The answer to the first question I leave to Professor James MacGregor Burns to explain in his excellent Foreword, and to whose theory of the Four Party System I completely subscribe. The answer to the second question provides the background and setting for the speeches on the Senate establishment which Senator Paul Douglas of Illinois and I made on the floor of the United States Senate on February 19, 20, and 21, 1963.

Rule XXIV of the Senate Rules, "Appointment of Committees," provides that the Senate "shall proceed by ballot to appoint severally the chairman of each committee, and then, by one ballot, the other members necessary to complete the same." The standing, or permanent legislative committees, are listed in rule XXV—sixteen of them from Aeronautical and Space Sciences to Rules and Administration—where the number of members of each committee, the jurisdiction of the committee, and the status of the committee (major or minor) are also all outlined. There is nothing in the rules about seniority. The number and particularly the size of the standing committees has varied greatly down through the years, and is in fact quite arbitrary. There is nothing in the rules to determine what the ratio between the two political parties shall be over-all or on specific committees. The general rule of thumb is that the number of majority and minority party seats on the committee shall reflect the relative strength in the Senate of the two parties. Thus, since there are sixty-seven Democrats and thirty-three Republicans in the Senate, the standing committees should have two Democratic for every one Republican member. The Majority Leader, however, has a great deal of discretion in deciding the size and ratio of individual committees in the allocation of the total number of committee assignments. Again, the rules say nothing about this.

Membership on the committee is determined by the respective parties as a party affair, with each party presenting an agreed slate to the Senate which is then ratified in accordance with rule XXIV. The ratios on the committees between the parties are determined actually by mutual agreement between the majority and minority leaders, plus the leaders of the Senate's ruling clique, sometimes known as the Establishment of the Inner Sanctum or the Club. The standing committees of the Senate form the backbone of the Senate itself since the committee structure or system is the basis of the Congressional process.

The question of how the parties determine which of their members shall serve on what Senate committees is, therefore, crucial. And the question of how and who of the majority and minority reach agreement on size and make-up of committees is also critical.

The Democratic party in the Senate—all those Senators who are elected from their respective states as Democrats—has given to a Steering Committee the power to make selections from among the Democratic Senators for service on the various committees. The Steering Committee is the Democratic Committee on Committees. Traditionally—and it is a tradition, nothing more, there is no Senate rule on these matters—members of the Steering Committee are named by the Majority Leader, the leader of the Democratic party in the Senate elected in a party caucus of all Democratic Senators. The Steering Committee has but two functions: (1) to give Democratic Senators their committee assignments, and (2) to determine the size and party ratio on each legislative committee. It meets, therefore ordinarily only once every two years,* at the beginning of a new Congress after a national election has changed the membership and party ratio of the Senate.

The system is virtually the same as was described by Senator La Follette of Wisconsin more than fifty years ago. (See pages 23 and 24.)

It is obvious, then, that the make-up of the Steering Committee itself is the key to both the size and make-up of all the Senate committees, and the key—in concert with the Committee on Committees of the Republican party—to the hierarchical structure of the Senate itself. It is also obvious that if the Steering Committee is to reflect accurately the actual total membership of the Democratic party in the Senate it must be representative of the geography and political philosophy of the Democratic Senators. In the Democratic party, where it is no secret that the views of Harry Flood Byrd and Hubert Horatio Humphrey are worlds apart, this is absolutely essential to democratic procedures.

In 1958 the electorate spoke loud and clear. The national Congressional elections amounted to a Democratic landslide, and the razor-thin margins by which the Democratic party constituted the dominant party in the 85th Congress were expanded to overwhelming majorities. To the Senate came fifteen new Democratic Senators, and also three new Republican Senators. All of them, in both parties, were twentieth-century men—moderate at the very least, on the whole young, mostly from the

---

* It will also meet from time to time to fill vacancies created by death or resignation.

industrialized and urban North, Midwest, and West, and without exception forward-looking. They made—from that day to this—a different place of the United States Senate. The American people appeared to have served notice that it was time for the Congress to move ahead, to begin to close the gap of political lag from which it had been suffering since the bipartisan conservative coalition had taken over control of the Congress in the late thirties. The elections of 1960 and 1962 further emphasized, albeit narrowly, this view.

The Steering Committee of the Democratic party at the time of that 1958 election was made up of fourteen members (including the Majority Leader, Majority Whip, and Party Secretary), of whom seven were from the South and seven were from the rest of the country. Prior to the election, that was not much out of line with the body of forty-nine Democratic Senators; but after election it was hardly representative of the sixty-two Democratic Senators. It was right after that election, in November of 1958, that I first called the attention of the (then) Majority Leader Lyndon Johnson to the need to reorganize the Steering Committee, and the need to revamp the institutional structure of the Democratic party in the Senate so that it would reflect not only the party within the Senate, and the will of the people as expressed in the election, but also the coming-of-age of the Senate in the modern world.

The Majority Leader did not agree with me; and he worked his will in the caucus.

In 1961, Mike Mansfield of Montana was elected Majority Leader. He made a commitment to the first Democratic Conference of the 87th Congress that the Steering Committee would reflect the ideology and geography of the entire membership of the Democratic party in the Senate—which after the 1960 elections consisted of sixty-four Senators, forty-two of them from outside the South. But though the Majority Leader appointed four non-Southerners to vacancies on the Steering Committee (including myself) as they occurred in the following two years, in 1963 the Steering Committee was still proportionally and philosophically out of balance, nine of the fifteen members being conservative. The only ways to correct that imbalance were for one or two Southern Senators on the committee to resign or to enlarge the committee. In the first Democratic Conference of the 88th Congress that issue was raised, but those of us who sought to enlarge the committee were defeated. As a result, the Steering Committee which made the assignments to committees for newly elected Democratic Senators and those Senators requesting changes in their assignments, was still not representative of the whole party in the Senate.

In an effort to make certain that the committee assignments to be made by the Steering Committee met with the approval of a majority of all the Democratic Senators, a motion was made by Senator Morse of Oregon in the first Democratic Conference of 1963 to require the approval of the conference itself of the committee assignments made by the Steering Committee. That, too, failed. The Steering Committee met and made its committee assignments in a manner which entrenched the control of the establishment over the committee structure of the Senate. I requested a Conference of Democratic Senators after the Steering Committee made its decisions in February, 1963, to review those decisions. The Majority Leader did not grant my request.

The only way then left to challenge the Steering Committee's decisions regarding committee assignments was by an appeal to the Senate itself under rule XXIV (cited above). The only way to challenge the agreements on the total size of committees, and the ratio of one party to another on those committees— agreements that had been reached by both parties in their respective caucuses by arrangement between the majority and minority leaders and carried into effect by the Democratic Steering Committee—was by an appeal to the Senate under rule XXV; in a word by amending the rules of the Senate.

How difficult this is, and what the real obstacles are in the path of bringing about needed reforms in the Senate's customs, traditions, and rules will be seen in the debate that follows. The speeches which Senator Douglas and I made in the Senate following the deliberations of the Democratic Steering Committee —on which I serve—were made before the Senate ratified the new committee assignments, and after I filed a number of amendments to rule XXV to change the size and make-up of a number of Senate committees in order to correct what I believed to be the injustices and inequities of what the Steering

Committee had done. Frankly, I had no hope of immediate success. But after some thought, and having been unable to arrange a party caucus, it seemed to me important and worthwhile to review publicly—as publicly as the Senate rules and the limitations of secrecy imposed on members of the Steering Committee permitted—what had happened in the Steering Committee, why I believed it was necessary to enlarge certain committees and change the party ratios in them, and finally to reiterate my repeated pleas for a thorough overhauling of the Senate rules.

Over the years I had found that the lack of democratic procedure within the party structures mirrored a lack of democratic procedure within the structure of the Senate itself. Procedure is the heart of justice, and strange as it may seem in a body dedicated to a government of laws, not of men, the procedures, customs, traditions, manners, and mores of the United States Senate are founded all too much on unwritten, unspoken, and largely unnoticed informal agreements among men. To the men who make these arrangements, who sincerely believe that the way the Senate is now run is the best way for it to be run, I have given the name the Senate establishment. (One could with equal validity include the House of Representatives and speak of the Congressional establishment.) I honor them for the sincerity of their views, but I strongly disagree with them. I believe that the Senate has become archaic, outmoded, obsolete as a meaningful democratic institution. If the Senate is to perform its constitutional role in the twentieth century, it must be changed to meet the needs of the twentieth century, and made capable of responding to the problems of the twentieth century. It would be neither so painful nor so difficult to modernize the Senate. I have suggested a number of reforms which would be useful. So have many others, in and out of the Senate.

Why, then, does the Senate not reform itself? Why is a situation permitted to exist in which a resolution approved by fifty-six Senators to change cloture—the famous rule XXII to shut off filibusters—from two-thirds to three-fifths of those Senators present and voting cannot be brought to a vote? The answer of the traditionalists, those who defend the present system, is that the Senate is the citadel of minority rights, the last stronghold against the tyranny of the majority. But the fact is our whole form of government, the tripartite constitutional system itself already has built-in all the checks and balances to tyranny that a modern government can afford without being incapable of action.

A Southern Senator who has said that "the South cannot afford the luxurious expense of two-partyism" is more candid in his explanation: "The last strength of States' rights is vested in the powers of your representatives in Washington whom you have elected, and reelected, and reelected. Their seniority is the source of your strength and power in Washington to preserve our States' rights."* States' rights is, generally speaking, the philosophy of the Senate establishment (of the Congressional Party, as Professor Burns so aptly puts it), a philosophy which neither political party has dared to take to the national electorate in a Presidential election in a generation, but which still prevails as a bipartisan conservative coalition in the Congress today. Indeed, the establishment is dedicated to the preservation of the status quo not only in the Senate, but in the country. That is why the establishment coalition resists change in the Senate rules and procedures—it is the last line of resistance against needed change in our society and our country. The Senate establishment is, in a word, the bulwark against democracy in the Senate, majority rule in the legislative branch of the government, and the will of the American people as expressed in national Presidential elections. These are, perhaps strong words. But I strongly believe them to be true.

So, too, do an increasing number of my colleagues, journalists, political scientists, and the public. The pattern which emerged so clearly from the committee assignments and party ratios' made in the Senate by both parties for the 88th Congress has not gone unnoticed. And though there are those who have wept and wrung their hands and clucked their tongues at having that pattern laid bare, it was necessary in the public interest to do so.

All during the course of this Congress I have continued my campaign for reform and modernization in the Senate, and an

---

* Olin Johnston of South Carolina, as reported in *U. S. News and World Report,* May 27, 1963.

increasing number of my colleagues are joining me in the endeavor. The Senate will not, in all likelihood, do what must be done in the 88th Congress. But as a result of the great racial crisis of 1963, with the help of the electorate in 1964, and a President concerned for the fate of his program in 1965—and perhaps his place in history—we may very well soon be successful. The Senate establishment's ability to keep the twentieth century from the door becomes every day a more difficult task. In view of our racial turmoil and unresolved economic and social problems at home and an unflinching and wily enemy abroad—able to act at a moment's notice—it should shortly be well-nigh impossible.

The poet laureate of the Senate establishment—and he is a fitting one—believes that the fall of the Senate establishment will be "the ultimate tragedy." Yet even he senses that it is coming. William S. White, author of *Citadel: The Story of the U.S. Senate,* wrote recently in his syndicated column:

> Perhaps it is too melancholy a fancy; but in bleak imagination one can hear the coming roll of the drums of threnody for another Appomattox—that Appomattox where the true sons of the South surrender the great sword of the Senate to carpetbaggers from abroad and scalawags from home.

As one whose grandfather fought and bled for the Confederacy but who still has some faith in democracy and in the people, I say: let the drums roll. The Founding Fathers would not have it otherwise.

Contents

February 19, 1963

MR. CLARK   Mr. President, I desire to address the Senate on the subject of the Senate establishment and how it operates. Perhaps the first thing to do is to state what I mean by "the Senate establishment." Senators may recall that last May, Richard Rovere, the very able reporter who writes for magazines such as the *New Yorker* and *Esquire*—since *Esquire* discarded its pin-up girls as the principal way of selling that magazine, and became a magazine for a little group of serious thinkers—wrote an article on the establishment of the United States; and in the article he compared those who he thought ran America—although I suspect that to some extent he had his tongue in his cheek—with the British establishment, which is headed by the royal family, and includes the peers, whether hereditary or only for life, and most of the aristocracy, if not the plutocracy, of Great Britain and Northern Ireland.

Mr. Rovere suggested that there was an ill-defined, but nonetheless clearly discernible, establishment in the United States. He proceeded to state the names of the persons whom he regarded as members of the establishment. His comments in that connection were quite interesting. For example, he stated that one of the two candidates for election to be President of the United States and to be Vice President of the United States would always be a member of the establishment, but the other one would not. He suggested that President Eisenhower was a member of the establishment, but that Vice President Nixon was not. Somewhat to my surprise, he concluded that Henry Luce was not a member of the establishment, but that Martin Luther King was —and so on, down the line.

It was a very entertaining article. Last summer I had occasion to commend it to my colleagues. Several of them told me they had read it, and they thanked me for calling it to their attention.

I believe that the concept of an establishment in America is something which all of us who try to understand the sometimes almost inexplicable ways in which we in this country act would do well to contemplate. Just as Great Britain has its establishment and the United States of America perhaps has its establishment, so, as I pointed out last year, the U.S. Senate has its establishment. I wish to discuss today what that establishment is, how it operates, and why in my opinion the present establishment is not operating in the interests of the future of the United States, or the future of the U.S. Senate, and certainly is not operating to the benefit of the future of the Democratic Party.

The Senate establishment, as I see it, after a relatively brief sojourn here—I am now in my seventh year—is almost the antithesis of democracy. It is not selected by any democratic process. It appears to be quite unresponsive to the caucuses of the two parties, be they Republican or Democratic. It is what might be called a self-perpetuating oligarchy with mild, but only mild, overtones of plutocracy. The way it operates is something like this:

There are a number of States, most of them Democratic, but one or two of them Republican, which inevitably and always return to the U.S. Senate members of one party, and under a custom which has grown up over the years of following the rule of seniority in making committee assignments, and in connection with the distribution of other perquisites of Senate tenure, the result has been that those who have been here longest have become chairmen of committees, and as such chairmen, have exercised virtual control over the distribution of favors, including committee assignments and other perquisites of office in the Senate, and largely—although not always, and not entirely, because there are exceptions—determine who shall be selected to posts of leadership in this body.

So far as individual members of the establishment are concerned, they are all good friends of mine. I hope they will continue to be good friends of mine after the present little misunderstanding between us is recorded on the ageless pages of the *Congressional Record* for the benefit of future historians. I honor those men. They are my friends. They are honest, intelligent, and, from the point of view of representing their States as opposed to the national interest, they are doing a fine job. I wish them long life, continued happiness, material prosperity, and spiritual peace—if not reelection. I do not know a single one whom I would oppose for reelection now if I were a citizen of his State. I prefer to leave that question to the citizenry of those States.

I hope that they would be as eager as I am to assure the reelection of certain Members of my party who desperately needed good committee assignments in order to shore up their campaigns for reelection next year. I regret that in a good many cases this sound principle was honored more in the breach than in the observance.

As I see it, the Senate establishment pretty well controls the assignment of Members to committees. How is that done? I think it is interesting to note that it is not only the present Senate establishment which does that. From time to time, going back at least to the early days of the present century, the same system prevailed. There have always been those who fought against the establishment, who thought that the Democratic caucus and the Republican caucus should determine who would select the members of committees and the other perquisites of office. One of the most eloquent men to speak in that vein was, at the time he spoke, a Republican. It was that very much revered and able Senator from Wisconsin, the elder Robert La Follette.

During the height of what was known as Aldrichism, referring to Nelson Aldrich, the eminent and conservative Senator from Rhode Island who left his mark for many years on the Senate, Senator La Follette said:

Under the present system of choosing the standing committees of the U.S. Senate a party caucus is called. A chairman is authorized to appoint a committee on committees. The caucus adjourns. The committee on committees is thereafter appointed by the chairman of a caucus. It proceeds to determine the committee assignments of Senators. This places the selection of the membership of the standing committees completely in the hands of a majority of the committee on committees, because in practice the caucus ratifies the action of the committee and the Senate ratifies the action of the caucus. See now what has happened: The people have delegated us to represent them in the Senate. The Senate, in effect, has delegated its authority to party caucuses upon either side. The party caucus delegates its authority to a chairman to select a committee on committees. The committee on committees largely defers to the chairman of the committee on committees in the final decision as to committee assignments. The standing committees of the Senate as selected determine the fate of all bills; they report, shape, or suppress legislation practically at will.

That is what Robert La Follette had to say about the Senate establishment in the days around 1905 to 1910 and thereafter when Nelson Aldrich was the undoubted Republican leader of the Senate establishment of that day.

It was true then, as it is now, that the establishment was bipartisan. The senior ranking members of the minority party are a part of the establishment; and they, in conference—usually informal, always friendly—with their colleagues on the other side of the aisle pretty well decide who is going to do what to whom.

That is what is happening in the Senate today. That is what has happened in the Senate many times before. But it does not always happen in the Senate, and it need not happen in the Senate much longer. Whenever it does happen in the Senate, in a constantly shrinking world, in which change is inevitable, I suggest that the existence of that kind of oligarchical rule is a detriment to the national interest.

There was a very famous occasion when the rank and file of the Senate membership overturned the establishment and in a couple of years passed legislation—which had long been bottled up in previous Senates—as important to the welfare of the country as almost any other program in the long sweep of history.

I shall relate what happened in 1913, after Woodrow Wilson

was elected President of the United States on a party platform which pledged to bring into legislative form the New Freedom —the program on which he defeated both William Howard Taft, seeking reelection to the Presidency, and Theodore Roosevelt, running on the Bull Moose ticket.

In 1913 the Democrats captured control of the Senate for the first time in 16 years. A majority of the Democratic Senators were progressive and espoused the progressive principles of the Baltimore platform, but the committee chairmanships and the important committee posts were to go to the conservative Democrats under the old seniority system in the Senate.

Note the striking analogy. A large majority of the Democratic Senators in the 88th Congress are also progressive. A majority of them support the Democratic platform adopted in Los Angeles in 1960. On that platform President Kennedy was swept into office by a very narrow majority.

We now stand at the beginning of the third session of what might be called a Kennedy Congress, but actually it is not a Kennedy Congress, and it seems to me that it is not going to be a Kennedy Congress. The principal reason why it is not going to be a Kennedy Congress, so far as the Senate is concerned, is, in my opinion, that we are operating under archaic, obsolete rules, customs, manners, procedures, and traditions—and because the operation under those obsolete and archaic setups is controlled by this oligarchical Senate establishment, a majority of the Members of which, by and large, are opposed to the program of the President.

I do not wish to overstate the case. There are able and effective Members of the establishment who will support the program of the President in many areas. There are a few Members of the establishment who will support the program of the President in some areas. But, by and large, the two-thirds majority of the Democratic Senators who are Kennedy men, and therefore liberals, and therefore want to get the country moving again, and therefore believe in the inevitability of change, are represented sparsely, if at all, in the Senate establishment.

I return now to a consideration of the situation of 1913. At that time, I point out again, the committee chairmanships and

the important committee positions would have gone to conservative Democrats under the old seniority system in the Senate. The
progressive Democrats, however, united to insure the passage of
their progressive legislation and modified the Senate rules to
aid in the translation of the Baltimore platform into legislation.

At that time there were 51 Democratic Senators, 44 Republicans, and 1 Progressive. Forty of the Democrats, 10 of the Republicans, and 1 Progressive—a total of 51—could be safely labeled
as in sympathy with the important planks of the Baltimore platform and of the policy of President Woodrow Wilson. I refer
to the currency, tariff, civil service reform, pure food, and health
planks.

In all, the progressives of the three parties had a very slim
majority in the Senate of 1913, but that majority was sufficient,
and it enabled the Democratic Senators, with the aid of their
Progressive colleague and of their friends in the Republican
Party, to set aside the seniority system in the Senate, to displace
senior committee chairmen, to replace the senior committee
chairmen with young men, some of whom had not served in
the Senate for more than 2 years; and, as a result of quiet meetings during different evenings in Washington they took over the
Senate, reconstituted the membership of all committees, got rid
of all the senior chairmen, and put their own men in.

A conference was held at Senator Luke Lea's home, to decide
on a caucus leader, one who would be able to reconcile the
differences with the conservative faction of the party and keep
it united in the Senate with the progressive faction. Thirty Senators were present at that meeting at Senator Lea's home, and
they agreed on John W. Kern, a Senator from Indiana with
only 2 years' tenure in the Senate. Positions on certain important committees were given to men who deserved them because
of seniority, but the memberships of various committees were
packed with progressives, regardless of their seniority, and on
several occasions the committee chairmen were themselves re-
placed. The old Senate procedures were changed to prevent a
committee chairman from halting legislation arbitrarily. Instead of only the chairman, a majority of the committee might

call the committee together at any time for consideration of a pending bill.

Mr. President, I have had before the Senate for the past 4 years a proposed rule which would do exactly that. It has been bottled up in the Committee on Rules and Administration. It has never seen the light of day.

In 1913 a majority of a majority of a committee was given power to name subcommittees to consider pending measures and to report to the full committee. I have had such a proposed rule pending in the Senate for the past 4 years, and it is still bottled up in the Committee on Rules and Administration.

A majority of a majority was given the power to name Members to confer with the House as to any bill over which the House and the Senate disagreed. I have had pending a proposed rule, bottled up in the Committee on Rules and Administration, which would accomplish the same result, although the text of the proposed rule is somewhat different.

The end results of the revolution of 1913 in the Senate of the United States were: First, emasculation of the old Senate seniority system; second, committee domination by the progressives, which meant the Wilson men; third, the Senate being democratized in terms of its rules and procedures; and fourth, the planks of the Baltimore platform being enacted into legislation.

I plead with my colleagues to do the same thing now—if not now, then next year—if not next year, then the year after—but let us get it done, while President Kennedy is still at the White House, if we want to preserve the Democratic Party for progressive principles, if we want to get the help of a number of our progressive friends on the Republican side—if we want to move this country forward and not be blocked by the hand of the past.

MR. DOUGLAS   Mr. President, will the Senator yield?

MR. CLARK   I yield to the Senator from Illinois.

MR. DOUGLAS   Is it not likely that, if it had not been for this successful revolution, in all probability the Federal Reserve System would not have been brought into being?

MR. CLARK   The Senator is quite correct. The establishment in those days had been opposed to the Federal Reserve System.

MR. DOUGLAS   Is it not likely that the Underwood tariff, which greatly reduced previous tariffs, would not have been put into effect?

MR. CLARK   I think that is quite correct.

MR. DOUGLAS   Is it not also likely that the Federal Trade Act would not have been passed?

MR. CLARK   The Senator is entirely correct.

MR. DOUGLAS   Is it not also true that, in all probability the other companion measure, dealing with unfair competitive practices, would not have been passed?

MR. CLARK   I believe that was the Clayton Act, which amended the Sherman Antitrust Act and put teeth into it.

MR. DOUGLAS   That is correct.

MR. CLARK   The Senator is correct.

MR. DOUGLAS   Is it not true that, in all probability, the Agricultural Credit Act would not have been passed?

MR. CLARK   I am confident the Senator is correct.

MR. DOUGLAS   In other words, the great domestic achievements of the Wilson administration from 1913 to 1915, before the war diverted the attention of the country from domestic reforms, would not have been possible had it not been for the procedural changes in the designation of committees by the rank and file of the Senators of the Democratic Party?

MR. CLARK   They were dependent upon modernization of the Senate procedures for committee makeup. I thank the Senator for the interjection.

Mr. President, it is interesting to note how closely analogous the situation in the Senate today is to that immediately following the election of President Wilson. This point I have made before, but I would like to quote from the report made by the Democratic steering committee of March 13, 1912:

> Your committee proposes certain reforms not only in the processes of the procedure in the Senate but in the political methods of our party in its organization. We propose that this great body shall be democratic not only in name but in practical reality, and that charges so often made that it is controlled by a few men through committee organization and otherwise shall never have any basis in fact.

For reasons which have never been disclosed to me, the minutes of the Democratic steering committee are under lock and key in the office of Mr. Robert Baker, the secretary of the majority.

It is true that any Senator is entitled to go there and look at those minutes. They make interesting reading, and I believe they should be made available to historians. No member of any Senator's staff is allowed to look at those minutes; and yet these are the public records of what the Democratic Party does in its conferences.

I am not suggesting that the minutes should be given to the press at the time they are taken. I am not suggesting that the proceedings of the Democratic conferences should not be behind closed doors. I think they should be. But I think, in due course, and after a reasonable time, the minutes should be made available to anybody who wants to see them, and particularly staff members of Senators who want to use those minutes in connection with matters pending before the Senate.

I hope that in the course of the next few years that relatively minor reform will be made. It should be made. I have urged it on both the former majority leader, now Vice President Johnson, and on the present majority leader, the Senator from Montana [Mr. Mansfield]. I honor and respect them. The present Vice President was a great leader, as is the present majority leader. I respect their decision not to make those minutes more freely available, but I must state in all candor that in my judgment, the decision is wrong. I hope that, in due course, we can persuade the leadership to reverse their position.

MR. MANSFIELD   Mr. President, will the Senator yield?

MR. CLARK   I yield.

MR. MANSFIELD   Because of circumstances over which I had no control, I came into the Chamber during the latter part of the Senator's remarks. May I ask to which minutes the Senator referred?

MR. CLARK   To the minutes of the Democratic conferences.

MR. MANSFIELD   The Senator wants those minutes made available even to staff members of a Senator. Is that correct?

MR. CLARK   I think they ought to be made available to the press.

MR. MANSFIELD   I would say that we ought to do away with closed party conferences—which I advocate, by the way—and have open hearings and invite the press and the public to them and bring our arguments and differences out into the open.

MR. CLARK I suggest to my friend in all candor that there is a middle ground which would be more effective and which I would advocate. I said, before the Senator came into the Chamber—and he did not hear me, of course—that I do not believe the minutes should be made immediately available to the press. I think an appropriate time, perhaps 3 months, 6 months, or a year, should elapse before the minutes are made available, but I think they are a part of the history of our times.

It seems to me perfectly absurd, when I want to ascertain what happened in the steering committee in 1913, that I have to go to Mr. Baker's office and get books unlocked, before I can read what happened at the time Mr. Wilson was in office. It makes no sense.

MR. MANSFIELD Of course, the conferences are supposed to be held in secret. It seems that what happens in those caucuses leaks out to the press very soon, within minutes, instead of after a lapse of 6 or 7 months or a year.

So far as concerns allowing a staff member of a Senator to look at confidential matters, based on what I have seen in my service in the Senate, all too often the assistants or members of the staff of a Senator are as important and influential as the Senator himself is. Those people are not elected. They do not go before the people. I think what is open only to a Senator should remain available only to the Senator himself.

MR. CLARK The Senator has made that point before in conversations in the past 2 years. I disagreed with him then. I disagree with him now. I see no great difference between allowing the staff members access to the minutes of the Democratic conferences and allowing staff members to have access to meetings of committees even if they are in executive session. After all, our proceedings are published in the *Congressional Record* every day. These are matters of history.

I would not open the conferences to the press. At the end of each session the majority leader briefs the press. Unfortunately, there have been leaks, and certain members have told the press what occurred. I agree with the Senator that there have been leaks, and that there should be none. But this is a part of American history. I am sorry the Senator does not agree with me. We agree on many other matters.

MR. MANSFIELD The Senator is frank. He has held to his opinion for a long time, to my personal knowledge, and he is entitled to that opinion. I felt, in all deference to the Senator, that I should reiterate my view on the subject.

So far as the Foreign Relations Committee is concerned—and I believe the Senator from Oregon will bear me out—we do not allow staff members in the executive meetings of the committee, and I do not think we should, because, I repeat, the staff members are not Senators who have been elected. They do not have the responsibilities which Senators have.

MR. CLARK I thank my friend for his statement, and reiterate my regret that I cannot agree with him.

To return to my subject, in 1961, and again this year, the Democratic conference approved a statement of the majority leader to the effect that the composition of the Democratic steering committee should reflect both the geographical distribution and the ideological views of Democratic Members of the Senate.

Speaking only for myself, as one of those who urged this position on the majority leader both in 1961 and 1963, I felt that that statement carried with it an implication that the size of the Democratic steering committee would be increased by sufficient numbers to make the committee representative of the whole membership of the Democratic members of the committee, or, in the alternative, of members of the committee from sections which were overrepresented from an ideological standpoint, in order to bring about the balance in geography and ideology which it seemed to me the approved statement indicated to be desired.

Efforts to increase the size of the committee, one sponsored by me, and one sponsored by the Senator from New Mexico [Mr. Anderson], were opposed by the Democratic leadership, and were therefore unsuccessful in a Democratic conference earlier this year.

MR. DOUGLAS Mr. President, will the Senator yield?

MR. CLARK I am glad to yield to my friend from Illinois.

MR. DOUGLAS Is it not true that prior to the establishment of the present steering committee, and prior to the death of Senator Chavez, of the 15 members on the steering committee only 1 was from any of the 12 States which lie between the Alleghenies and the Rockies and can be described as the East and West Central States?

MR. CLARK The Senator is correct. I intended to develop that point in some detail, if he will permit me to do so.

MR. DOUGLAS I am sorry for the interruption.

MR. CLARK I hope the Senator will listen carefully to what I have to say, and interject if there is anything that he would like to add to what I have to say.

At the beginning of this year the steering committee consisted of 14 members. There was one vacancy, because for some years, but not always, the committee had consisted of 15 members. As recently as 1946 there were 17 members on the Democratic steering committee. I had been hopeful that the committee would be increased to at least that number this year. I myself sponsored a motion to increase it to 19, feeling it would be better to have a large committee with adequate geographical and ideological representation rather than to attempt to get members from over-represented areas to resign. As of the early part of January of this year, the steering committee consisted of the following members: Senator Mansfield of Montana, Chairman; Senator Humphrey, of Minnesota, whip; Senator Smathers, Florida, secretary; Senator Bible, Nevada; Senator Clark, Pennsylvania; Senator Dodd, Connecticut; Senator Ellender, Louisiana; Senator Hayden, Arizona; Senator Holland, Florida; Senator Johnston, South Carolina; Senator McClellan, Arkansas; Senator Robertson, Virginia; Senator Russell, Georgia; Senator Williams, New Jersey.

Senators Dodd, Williams of New Jersey, and Clark had been added in 1961, which somewhat diluted but did not eliminate the very heavy overrepresentation of certain areas and certain philosophies, or the underrepresentation of others.

As a result of a rather spirited discussion and as a result of the failure of efforts to increase the size of the committee, first to 19, and later on motion of the Senator from New Mexico [Mr. Anderson], to 17, the committee was left at 15, and the 1 vacancy was filled by the appointment of the Senator from

Illinois [Mr. Douglas]. As a result, there are now on the committee 7 out of 15 members from the South, including both Senators from Florida. These Senators are: Smathers, Ellender, Holland, Johnston, McClellan, Robertson, and Russell. There are 23 southern Senators—34 percent of the Democratic membership of the Senate. I include in the South Oklahoma and Arkansas. Sometimes they are a little difficult to identify, but I put them in the South not only because of geography but also, to some extent, ideology.

Therefore, 47 percent of the total membership of the steering committee comes from those 13 States.

If we were to be guided solely on the basis of geography, this section of the country would be entitled to five seats. I point out that without exception these able, charming, friendly Senators from the South, all of whom are good friends of mine, belong to the conservative wing of the Senate Democratic Party. There are three Senators from the Northeast, Clark, Dodd, and Williams of New Jersey, out of 13 northeastern Senators, representing 9 of the 12 Northeastern States. To my regret the Democrats have no Senators from the other three Northeastern States. These Senators are all members of the liberal wing of the Democratic Party.

There are three Senators from the Pacific and Mountain States —Senators Bible, Hayden, and Mansfield—out of 17 western Senators representing 12 of the 13 Western States. Two of these three Senators, I believe they would agree, are proud members of the conservative wing of the Democratic Party. The other member, the distinguished and able majority leader, is a follower of the President of the United States and of the liberal wing of our party.

As a result of the succession of the Senator from Illinois [Mr. Douglas] to the committee, there are now two Senators from the Midwest, both of them liberals, Senators who support our President, almost always—Senators Humphrey and Douglas—out of 15 Senators representing 9 of the 12 Middle Western States.

MR. DOUGLAS   Mr. President, will the Senator yield further?

MR. CLARK   I am happy to yield to my friend from Illinois.

MR. DOUGLAS   When I first came to the Senate, in 1949, there was only 1 Democrat from those 12 States, Senator Lucas, of Illinois. We have gained 14 seats since then, so there are now, I believe, 15 Democratic Senators from these States. Indeed, the great gains which the Democratic Party has made since the election of 1946 have been largely and almost exclusively from what is roughly known as the Mississippi Valley, from the territory drained by the Mississippi River and its tributaries. And yet up until a few days ago we had but one representative on the steering committee.

MR. CLARK   If the Senator will permit me to make an interjection at this point, the Senator from Illinois is correct. There are 15 from the Middle West.

MR. DOUGLAS   I appreciate that comment. Prior to the last selection, which I must admit came as a great surprise to me, there was only one representative on the steering committee from the Middle West, which on a geographical basis within our party was the most underrepresented area in the Nation. It is still underrepresented.

MR. CLARK   The Senator is correct.

Turning from geography to ideology, and to recapitulate, of the 15 members on the committee, there are 9 whom, I am confident, any objective observer would classify as conservative: Senators Smathers, Bible, Ellender, Hayden, Holland, Johnston, McClellan, Robertson, and Russell. They are proud to call themselves conservative. That is a fine name. It has come down through the history of all countries through the ages. There is nothing wrong with being conservative. It just happens to be a fact that these Senators are conservatives.

According to my count—and some may differ one way or the other—there are at most 27 conservative Democrats out of 67 Democrats in the entire Senate; so 9 out of 15 Senators who are members of the vital committee which selects committee members are from the conservative ranks of our party, and only 6 from the liberal wing, the Kennedy wing, the modern wing, which numbers, at a minimum, 40—and I should say more nearly 45—of the 67 Democratic Members of the Senate. Those six are Senators Mansfield, Humphrey, Dodd, Douglas, Williams of New Jersey, and Clark.

As I have said, efforts to change this situation in the Democratic conference failed. They failed largely, I think, because the leadership announced against it and spoke against it in conference and threw the full impact of its undoubted moral authority against what, to me at least, seems to be this badly needed reform.

I suggest in all candor that, as a result of this action, the present membership of the steering committee accordingly does not fairly represent either the geography or the ideology of the Democratic Members of the Senate. It does not carry into effect the statement approved by the Democratic conference 2 years ago and again this year to the effect that the composition of the Democratic steering committee should reflect both the geographical distribution and the ideological views of the Democratic Members of the Senate. In point of fact, it does neither.

Whom does the steering committee of the Democratic Party represent? It represents the Democratic side of the establishment. It represents those who hold the positions of committee chairmen. Senator Mansfield has recently resigned as chairman of the Committee on Rules and Administration. His resignation was effective a few days ago.

Senator Bible is chairman of the Committee on the District of Columbia. Senator Ellender is chairman of the Committee on Agriculture and Forestry. Senator Hayden is chairman of the Committee on Appropriations. Senator Johnston is chairman of the Committee on Post Office and Civil Service. Senator McClellan is chairman of the Committee on Government Operations. Senator Robertson is chairman of the Committee on Banking and Currency. Senator Russell is chairman of the Committee on Armed Services.

I do not make these comments in criticism of those Senators. Far from it. All I say is that they exemplify the same situation, to my way of thinking—the same unsound situation—which confronted Robert La Follette when he made his fight for the democratization of the Senate in the days before the Wilson administration, and Senator John Kern and the other Wilson men when they made their successful fight against the same situation in the Senate in 1913, a successful fight which resulted in the passage of the New Freedom legislation.

Let us see what the Senate establishment in control of the steering committee has done to Members of the Senate who are not on that committee and who, one would think, should be entitled by the rule of seniority to assignments to committees on which they desired to serve. Let us see what the assignments which were made do to the program of the President of the United States.

I am bound by a pledge of secrecy which I shall keep, not to reveal the votes within the steering committee. I have no pledge not to reveal the results; indeed, the results are a matter of public record. I have no pledge not to reveal Senators who desired assignments to committee seats to which one would think they were entitled, or not to point out that seniority was ignored in refusing them those seats.

To my mind, this is important, because several of the Senators who were denied committee seats to which by seniority they were entitled are facing bitter and possibly uphill odds in their efforts to get reelected to the Senate next year. One would think that the steering committee would have been anxious to help those Senators by giving them positions of prestige, on the committees, prestige which they needed, so as to assist them in their campaigns before the people of their States for reelection in the fall of 1964. Yet on nine committees, ignoring seniority, the requests of those Senators were overridden, and Senators having far less seniority, and not required to face the electorate for another 6 years, were given choice committee seats, seats which rarely in the past have gone to freshmen Senators.

MR. MANSFIELD   Mr. President, will the Senator from Pennsylvania yield?

MR. CLARK   I am happy to yield.

MR. MANSFIELD   I think that the record ought to show that it is not exactly true that "rarely in the past" have freshman Senators received coveted assignments. As a matter of fact, when I first came to the Senate, in 1952, I was assigned to the Committee on Foreign Relations. The Senator from Missouri [Mr. Symington] was placed on the Committee on Armed Services. The Senator from Washington [Mr. Jackson] was assigned to the Committee on Interior and Insular Affairs. The former

Senator from Texas, Mr. Daniel, was placed on the Committee on the Judiciary. Senator Kennedy was assigned to the Committee on Labor and Public Welfare. The Senator from Tennessee [Mr. Gore] was assigned to the Committee on Public Works. As I recall, the Senator from Tennessee did not receive one of the assignments which he wished at that time. That situation was corrected later.

So far as new Senators are concerned, I point out—and I have said this many times—that in this body the newest Member is the equal of the oldest Member and is entitled to just as much consideration. I recognize an occasional application of the principle of seniority. On the basis of seniority, I voted for the distinguished senior Senator from Wisconsin [Mr. Proxmire] on the first committee assignment which was before us; namely, the Committee on Appropriations. The Senator from Wisconsin received only one vote, and that was my vote. I so voted because the Senator from Wisconsin told me that the Committee on Appropriations was his second choice, and I was taking no chances on his receiving at least one preferred committee. I also voted for his assignment to the Committee on Finance, because I felt he was entitled to that position. I do not care if the record shows it; it is the truth.

I do not believe we ought to downgrade the new Senators. I think they are an excellent group of men. I am delighted that they are on our side.

But I call the attention of the Senate to this fact: The Senator from Indiana [Mr. Bayh] asked to be assigned to the Committee on the Judiciary and the Committee on Public Works. He received both assignments.

The Senator from Maryland [Mr. Brewster] asked to be assigned to the Committee on Public Works and the Committee on Post Office and Civil Service. He received both of those assignments, and also an assignment to the Committee on Government Operations.

So far as I know, the Senator from Oklahoma [Mr. Edmondson] asked for assignment only to the Committee on Aeronautical and Space Sciences. He was given an assignment to that committee; and also—without his acquiescence or knowledge—we gave him an assignment to the Committee on Agriculture and Forestry.

The Senator from Hawaii [Mr. Inouye] requested assignment to the Committee on Armed Services and the Committee on Public Works. He got both.

The Senator from Massachusetts [Mr. Kennedy] requested assignment to the Committee on the Judiciary and the Committee on Commerce. We gave him one of his two choices; namely, assignment to the Committee on the Judiciary; and he was also given an assignment to the Committee on Labor and Public Welfare.

The Senator from South Dakota [Mr. McGovern] requested assignment to the Committee on Agriculture and Forestry and the Committee on Interior and Insular Affairs. We gave him both.

The Senator from New Hampshire [Mr. McIntyre] applied for assignment to the Committee on Banking and Currency and the Committee on Government Operations. He was given both assignments, and also was given an assignment to the Committee on the District of Columbia.

The Senator from Wisconsin [Mr. Nelson] asked for assignment to the Committee on Public Works and the Committee on Interior and Insular Affairs. He got both assignments.

The Senator from Connecticut [Mr. Ribicoff] asked for assignment to the Finance Committee and to the Committee on Government Operations. He received both assignments.

I do not think we have any apologies to make for these assignments; and I am delighted that, by and large, we were able to give these new Members the assignments they sought.

I am only sorry that the two Senators who got only one of the two committee assignments they sought were not treated in the way the others were—in other words, were not given both the committee assignments they sought.

Now we come to some other committee assignments, because other committee assignments were made by the steering committee. I was voted an assignment to the Appropriations Committee. Let me say that I wrote to all the members of the steering committee—including the Senator from Pennsylvania, but not including the Senator from Illinois, who at that time was not on the committee—and asked for their support.

MR. CLARK Let me say that I voted for assignment of the Senator from Montana to that committee.

MR. MANSFIELD I know the Senator from Pennsylvania did; and I am happy to say that the vote was unanimous, because I voted for myself. [Laughter.]

The Senator from Alaska [Mr. Bartlett] was selected by the steering committee for assignment to the Appropriations Committee; the Senator from Ohio [Mr. Young], for assignment to the Armed Services Committee; the Senator from Nevada [Mr. Cannon], for assignment to the Commerce Committee; the Senator from Michigan [Mr. Hart], for assignment to the Commerce Committee; the Senator from Florida [Mr. Smathers], for assignment to the Foreign Relations Committee; the Senator from Rhode Island [Mr. Pell], for assignment to the Committee on Government Operations; and the Senator from Arizona [Mr. Hayden], the President pro tempore of the Senate, was assigned —at his specific request, and, I think, based on seniority, as well as other things—to the Committee on Interior and Insular Affairs.

The Senator from Wyoming [Mr. McGee] was assigned to the Committee on Post Office and Civil Service.

The Senator from North Carolina [Mr. Jordan] was assigned to the Committee on Public Works; and the Senator from West Virginia [Mr. Byrd] was assigned to the Committee on Rules and Administration.

The Senator from Pennsylvania [Mr. Clark] received the overwhelming endorsement of the steering committee for assignment to the Committee on Rules and Administration, as well.

MR. CLARK Mr. President, if the Senator from Montana will yield, let me say that, as I recall, that vote was rather close, and I just squeaked through—with the help, I have no doubt, of the Senator from Montana, although perhaps he may not wish to state how he voted.

MR. MANSFIELD I may say that I voted twice for the Senator from Pennsylvania. [Laughter.]

MR. CLARK Mr. President, I have no quarrel with what the

majority leader has said. He has recited accurately a part—but not all—of the story about what happened in the steering committee. I have no quarrel with giving freshman Senators fine committee assignments. In fact, I endorse the rule—which I believe was first put into effect by the Vice President, when he was majority leader—that every new Democratic Senator should receive at least one good committee assignment, before any more senior Democratic Senator receives two good committee assignments.

Today there are, by reason of the passage of time and various other things, 14 Democratic Senators who have 3 major committee assignments. Probably that is due to the wisdom of the voters in returning by large majorities Democratic Senators to the Senate. So there are more of us than there used to be. But I would be the last to say that freshman Senators should not receive the best committee assignments which are available to them; and I endorse the principle that seniority should be ignored, in order to give each freshman Senator at least one good major committee assignment. In fact, at that meeting it would have been possible to give almost every freshman Senator two major committee assignments.

At any rate, I propose to call the roll; and I think it will then be very obvious that certain Senators with seniority, and who are faced with hard races for reelection, were not treated with the generosity which I had hoped they would receive from their colleagues.

I now continue to point out what happened in the steering committee—although I shall keep my pledge not to reveal the votes, except to the extent that perhaps I was seduced into doing so, inasmuch as I wished to inform all concerned that I had voted for the majority leader.

When the Democratic steering committee met, it became obvious that in filling committee membership vacancies, the establishment would ignore seniority when to ignore it would strengthen the establishment's control, but would follow it when to do so would have the same result. Thus, in making committee assignments, seniority was ignored—in filling the vacancies on the following eight committees: Aeronautical and

Space Sciences, Appropriations, Armed Services, Finance, Interior and Insular Affairs, Judiciary, Public Works, and Rules and Administration.

However, in three cases seniority was followed; namely, in making the assignments to the Committee on Foreign Relations, the Commerce Committee, and the Committee on Public Works. I ask Senators to note that seniority was followed in making assignments to the Committee on Public Works, in order to assure the appointment of a southerner; and seniority was ignored in order to prevent the appointment of a northerner.

I should like to discuss those committee assignments seriatim, and I shall do so alphabetically.

There was one vacancy on the Committee on Aeronautical and Space Sciences. The membership ratio for that committee was 10 Democrats to 5 Republicans, and the ratio was not changed. The applicants for assignment to the committee, in their order of seniority, were Senators Sparkman, Monroney, Byrd of West Virginia, Moss, Inouye, Bayh, Edmondson, and Nelson. Under the rule adopted by the steering committee prior to the time when it voted to fill the vacancies, Senators Sparkman, Monroney, and Byrd of West Virginia, were ineligible, because they already had two major committee assignments, and to give them a third one would violate the changed rule that, except to the extent of a "grandfather" clause, which I shall explain later on— they were not entitled to a third major committee assignment. That meant that the Senator from Utah [Mr. Moss]—who will go into a reelection campaign in 1964, one which I am sure he expects to be very close, indeed; and I see him on the floor at this time, and I am sure he will agree; however, I state that all of us hope he will succeed—would have been, on a seniority basis, entitled to assignment to the Committee on Aeronautical and Space Sciences. However, by a very substantial vote he was denied that assignment, in favor of my good friend, the Senator from Oklahoma [Mr. Edmondson], whose seniority was below not only that of the Senator from Utah [Mr. Moss], but also that of the Senator from Hawaii [Mr. Inouye] and the Senator from Indiana [Mr. Bayh]. I suggest that it was not in the interest of the Democratic Party, and certainly it was not in the interest of the Senator from Utah [Mr. Moss], and it was not in the interest of the rule of seniority which the establishment so rigorously follows on other occasions, to bypass the Senator from Utah [Mr. Moss], and thus deny him the assignment he sought— namely, to the Committee on Aeronautical and Space Sciences.

The next committee is Agriculture and Forestry. I am telling no tales out of school when I say that there was practically a rush. I dislike to compare it to the rush of the Gadarene swine. Of course, the comparison is inadequate. But there was a rush such as cattle in a stampede to get off the Committee on Agriculture and Forestry. On that committee were four Senators who wanted to get off, and only one Senator—I presume somewhat reluctantly—was willing to go on. So there was no contest in respect to that situation. A junior Senator must be drafted against his will—sort of hog-tied or bulldozed—to get him on the Committee on Agriculture and Forestry in order to let a couple of other Senators off who wished to get off. So no problem of seniority was there.

I see the distinguished Senator from South Dakota [Mr McGovern] in the chair. If I have misstated his position, and if he was zealous, keen, and anxious to go on the Committee on Agriculture and Forestry, I know that he will correct the record when he has an opportunity to leave the chair.

MR. MANSFIELD   Mr. President, will the Senator yield?

MR. CLARK   I am happy to yield.

MR. MANSFIELD   I am delighted that the distinguished junior Senator from South Dakota [Mr. McGovern] is the Presiding Officer of the Senate at this moment. I was called from the Chamber in response to a telephone call.

I hope the Senator from Pennsylvania [Mr. Clark] will make clear to the Senate that the distinguished Senator from South Dakota [Mr. McGovern] was an assiduous and determined volunteer for the Committee on Agriculture and Forestry. So far as the Senator from Oklahoma [Mr. Edmondson] was concerned, he was not a volunteer, but we thought it best in the interest of all concerned that he be lassoed and put on that committee.

MR. CLARK   I think I have already stated that.

I turn now to the Committee on Appropriations. The prize

committees in the Senate historically are Appropriations, Finance, Armed Services, and Foreign Relations. To be sure, individual Senators may prefer assignments to other committees. But those are the key prize committees on which almost any Senator would like to serve. I think that is proved by the number of applications for those committees as compared to the almost frightening lack of applications for other committees whose work is most important to the appropriate operation of the Senate.

When we come to the Committee on Appropriations, there were 10 applicants for 2 vacancies. There were two vacancies.

I point out that at an earlier stage of the negotiations between the majority and the minority leaders and their able representatives, Mr. Baker and Mr. Trice, it had been thought that the size of the Appropriations Committee might well be increased from 27 to 29, and the ratio changed from 17 Democrats and 10 Republicans to 19 Democrats and 10 Republicans, in order to avoid "bumping," as the expression goes, any Republican Senator off a committee on which he then served.

It is true that historically—many times in the past—Senators, having served, have been so "bumped." Having become available as members of a particular committee, they are nonetheless required to remove themselves from further deliberations of that committee by either resigning or being "kicked off" in order that the ratio of Democrats and Republicans on particular committees could be in total and in general in proportion to the number of Democratic and the number of Republican Senators.

Perhaps I should interject now to say that I am proud to say that, as a result of the elections last November, the Democratic majority in the Senate was increased from 64 to 67 percent by the addition of three more Democrats, and that, in turn, imposed a moral obligation—not under any rule—to see that the ratio of seats as between Democrats and Republicans should be pretty close to 67 percent for Democrats and 33 percent for Republicans.

What I am trying to say—and I suspect that I was not as clear as I thought I was—is that when we add up the total of available committee seats, the percentage of Democratic seats should be 67 percent and the percentage of Republican seats should be 33 percent. The 67 percent is an increase from the 64 percent which prevailed in the preceding Congress.

We can make such changes in any number of ways. We can make them in committees of the Senate like Finance, Armed Services, and Appropriations, or we can make them in other committees as to which no one is very excited, in connection with which there are no controversial matters, and where the program is not keenly affected by the ratio of Republicans to Democrats in the Senate. I for one would have made those changes where the important issues are at stake, and where the program of the President is in jeopardy.

But, no; the decision in key instances was not to do that. I make no charges and attribute no motives to any Senator. I am not one who would say that there is any ulterior motive of any sort in what was done. Let the record speak for itself. The only Senator "bumped off" a committee was the Senator from New York [Mr. Javits]. He was "bumped off" the Committee on Appropriations because a recommendation which had been made theretofore became politically unfeasible, and the status of the committee was not changed, as it had been originally hoped it could be, to 29 members, with a 19 to 10 ratio, but was fixed at an 18 to 9 ratio.

I should like to reiterate. I charge no Senator with wrongful motivation. I merely point to the fact that the only Senator "bumped off" any committee this time was the Senator from New York.

MR. MANSFIELD   Mr. President, will the Senator yield?

MR. CLARK   I am happy to yield.

MR. MANSFIELD   What the Senator has said is true. But I assure the Senator from New York [Mr. Javits] of something he already knows. There was nothing personal attached to the action of the Steering Committee. While the Senator from Pennsylvania quotes the *Record,* nevertheless there is an implication. I wish to say for the *Record* that I would have been willing to increase the membership of the committee by two members so that the Senator from New York could have remained on it, if at the same time the leadership on the other side had been willing to increase the membership of the Finance Committee by two. But, so far as going all the way is concerned, I would be lax in my duty. I would personally have considered a quid pro quo. But I assure the Senator from New York nothing personal was involved. He knows this. It was a matter of political arithmetic. That was the only thing we could do under the circumstances. So long as the Senator's name has been mentioned, and the Senator from Pennsylvania has been stating a fact, I hope that no inference will be drawn from the fact that the Senator from Pennsylvania, as a member of the steering committee, was present during all the considerations of that committee and is fully aware of the facts.

But so long as such implications are again being made, I wish to say, speaking personally, that it is my hope that from now on all the meetings of the steering committee, the policy committee, and the Democratic caucus will be held in the open and not behind closed doors, because so far as the Democrats are concerned, secrecy is becoming an unknown quantity.

(At this point Mr. Edmondson took the chair as Presiding Officer.)

MR. CLARK Let me ask my friend from Montana a question.

MR. MANSFIELD Yes.

MR. CLARK I thought I was maintaining the ground rules in this speech. Is it not correct to say that I came to the Senator from Montana and said to him, at the conclusion of the meeting. "Mike, to what extent are these matters we have discussed confidential?" And the Senator from Montana said to me, "Joe, you should not tell what any vote was. For the rest, there is no inhibition."

MR. MANSFIELD That is correct. I said that, but I had hoped that there would be a certain amount of discretion in any debate or discussion concerning what the steering committee did.

I do not like to bring out how I voted on certain matters. I am sure the Senator from Pennsylvania does not, either. But in view of the fact that this matter is being gone into in some detail, I feel that I am within my rights in telling the Senator from Wisconsin [Mr. Proxmire], for example, how I voted insofar as he was concerned on two particular committees, and I feel within my rights in telling the Senator from Pennsylvania [Mr.

Clark] that I voted for him twice when he, in effect, dragged the admission out of me.

MR. CLARK I thank the Senator from Montana. I hope he does not accuse me of a lack of discretion. I know he does not mean to.

MR. JAVITS rose.

MR. CLARK I yield to the Senator from New York.

MR. JAVITS Mr. President, I am deeply interested in what is going on. This is the second time today that this matter has been discussed as it relates to me. However, in view of the fact that the Senator from Pennsylvania, who to me is one of the most respected and useful Members of this body, is discussing an intraparty problem—

MR. CLARK If the Senator will yield, I shall come in a few moments to the interparty aspects of it.

MR. JAVITS I would not wish to intrude upon his analysis of the facts with some independent statement of my own. I expressed myself earlier today as one who philosophically accepted the situation as he found it, and although I can understand the speculations of others, I chose rather to say merely, "This is political, and there will be another day."

If the Senator will yield to me, I should like to make a brief statement, putting the matter in focus for myself, either when the Senator from Pennsylvania has concluded or now, if it would be possible to print my remarks at the end of his statement, because I would not wish to intrude upon his statement at all and I would rather make my own independently. If it is preferable, I will wait until the Senator has concluded.

MR. CLARK If the Senator presses me to yield, I will yield. I hope to be through in about 15 minutes.

MR. JAVITS I would rather wait.

MR. CLARK Mr. President, I return to a consideration of the Appropriations Committee and the condition having to do with applications from the Democrats for membership on that committee.

I may point out that there was an initial suggestion, which received very favorable consideration, coming from the leadership, that the size of that committee should be increased to 29 and that the ratio should be made 19 to 10. Had that been the case not only would the Senator from New York [Mr. Javits] have retained his seat, but also one more Democrat, desperately anxious to get on that committee to help him in his campaign for reelection, would have been selected.

The order of seniority for that committee, in terms of applications, for the 10 Senators applying for seats, was as follows: Mansfield, Yarborough, Proxmire, Engle, Bartlett, Hart, Moss, Long of Missouri, Brewster, and Inouye.

As I think was perfectly appropriate, the committee unanimously appointed the majority leader to a seat which he desired and to which he was entitled on the basis of seniority. It then proceeded to elect the Senator from Alaska [Mr. Bartlett] to the other vacancy, ignoring the prior seniority claims of the Senator from Texas [Mr. Yarborough] and the Senator from Wisconsin [Mr. Proxmire], and, with equal seniority, the claim of the Senator from California [Mr. Engle].

I yield to no man in my admiration for the Senator from Alaska. He is a marvelous Senator. He represents his State with the greatest of fidelity. He is a good and warm friend, and I respect and honor him, but of all Senators who will come up for reelection next year I do not know of any other who will have less opposition than my good friend the Senator from Alaska.

MR. LONG of Louisiana. Mr. President, will the Senator yield for a question?

MR. CLARK I am happy to yield.

MR. LONG of Louisiana Is the Senator suggesting that Members should be assigned to committees based on their prospects for being reelected?

MR. CLARK My point is very clear, I say to the Senator from Louisiana. I think there is an obligation on the part of the Democratic steering committee, other things being equal—and they were in this case—not to ignore the prior seniority claims of Senators who are about to engage in very difficult campaigns for reelection, in order to put on a committee a junior Senator —not a freshman Senator seeking a first assignment to a good committee, but a junior Senator—whose needs are not as great, and, I would say, though perhaps others will disagree, whose competence for the committee on which he wants to serve is no higher, although it is very great, than that of other Senators seeking the same position.

MR. LONG of Louisiana   Mr. President, if the Senator will pardon me for a personal reference, I came to this body after having been elected by a margin of one-half of 1 percent of the vote, for a 2-year term. When I was assigned my committee seat I did not get any committee in which I had expressed an interest. As a matter of fact, 17 other Senators who came after I came got their committee assignments first.

MR. CLARK   The Senator has done pretty well by now.

MR. LONG of Louisiana   Because some die and some are defeated.

MR. MANSFIELD   And some retire.

MR. LONG of Louisiana   The practical effect of it all was that no one was concerned about the fact that the other 17 Senators had 6 years to serve before they had to run for reelection.

MR. DOUGLAS   Mr. President, will the Senator yield?

MR. LONG of Louisiana   I have seen other Senators "bumped off" committees because of a change in membership, yet I have never heard them complain or suggest that the committee should be enlarged because of it.

MR. CLARK   The Senator has not heard them complain yet. I am complaining for them.

MR. LONG of Louisiana   I see. Generally speaking, after more than 14 years of service in this body, I do not know of any Senator who was any more discriminated against than this Senator when he came to the Senate; but, generally speaking, it seems to me that most of the Senators who have had to be "bumped" from a committee have taken it graciously and said, "Those are the fortunes of politics. We lost some seats on our side of the aisle."

MR. CLARK   I do not know of any Senator who is not taking it graciously. The Senator has not heard any complaints from the Senators who are involved. The Senator is hearing my complaint on their behalf, and I am not even authorized to complain on their behalf, but I am just doing it.

MR. DOUGLAS Mr. President, will the Senator yield?

MR. CLARK I am happy to yield.

MR. DOUGLAS As the Senator from Louisiana knows, I hold him not only in esteem but also in affection. I am very proud to serve with him on the Committee on Finance. I am extremely pleased that he is up in the driver's seat, at the right hand of the throne, occupying the No. 2 position on the Finance Committee.

As I look down the roster of the Committee on Foreign Relations, I observe that out of a total of 11 Democratic members the Senator from Louisiana ranks sixth. He is No. 6 on that committee, occupying the central position.

I rejoice in the rewards which have been given to him and which he richly deserves, but he should not weep bitter tears over the discrimination which has been practiced against him. It does not exist. He has done extremely well.

MR. LONG of Louisiana This Senator is not weeping about any discrimination.

MR. DOUGLAS I am glad.

MR. LONG of Louisiana He simply makes the point that this Senator has never received anything in this body except on the basis of seniority, and in at least 20 cases I could cite, if the Senator wanted me to do so, another Senator got a committee assignment notwithstanding this Senator's seniority. I am not complaining about it. I feel that if a Senator does his job and is regarded well enough to be reelected, he will eventually obtain a seat on any committee by seniority. I have deliberately stepped aside and agreed to allow other Members of the Senate to go on certain committees, notwithstanding that I had more seniority.

I do not see what the Senator is accomplishing by suggesting this reform to suit his views, because, with 100 Members in the Senate, I suppose each one of them would have his own ideas about how to organize the committees which would justify placing almost any Senator on a committee ahead of another Senator.

MR. CLARK Is my friend suggesting that we should have a gag rule and that I should stop before I complete my statement?

MR. LONG of Louisiana No. I merely make this point: Dropping a Senator from a committee has happened many times during the 14 years I have been in the Senate. The Senator is making the first speech I have heard complaining that that should not have happened and inferring that it was unfair and improper. The law provides how the problem should be handled. The Senator from Louisiana has been trying to be guided by the law and by the seniority system.

MR. CLARK   Mr. President, turning now to the Appropriations Committee, I point out that the seniority system with regard to the Appropriations Committee was ignored by bypassing Senators Yarborough and Proxmire and giving the coveted seat to the Senator from Alaska [Mr. Bartlett], when Senators Engle and Hart, both of whom have difficult election campaigns coming up, are of equal seniority with the Senator from Alaska.

MR. MC GOVERN   Mr. President, will the Senator yield?

MR. CLARK   I yield.

MR. MC GOVERN   A few minutes ago, when the Senator was referring to the assignment to the Committee on Agriculture and Forestry, I think he gave the impression that I was assigned to that committee somewhat against my will.

MR. CLARK   I did not mean to do so, because the Senator was an applicant and his name was on the list.

MR. MC GOVERN   I think the *Record* should show that, while I appreciate the statement of the Senator from Pennsylvania that the problems of agriculture are frustrating and sometimes painful, nevertheless agriculture is still the most important single industry in the Nation, and certainly of overwhelming importance in my State. I asked for assignment to the Committee on Agriculture and Forestry, as well as the Committee on Interior and Insular Affairs. I am happy that both of those requests were granted, but I appreciate the statement the Senator from Pennsylvania is making.

MR. CLARK   I am confident that our friend from South Dakota will make a substantial contribution to the solution of the excruciatingly difficult problems which confront the farmers of our country, and I admire his courage for being willing and anxious to undertake the task.

Having noted that seniority was ignored for the second time in connection with the Appropriations Committee, having been ignored for the first time in connection with the Aeronautical and Space Sciences Committee, I now turn to the Committee on Armed Services. In that case the ratio was changed from 11 Democrats and 6 Republicans to 12 Democrats and 5 Republicans. The applicants for assignment to that committee, in order of seniority, were Young of Ohio, Hart, Moss, McIntyre, Brewster, and Inouye; Brewster and Inouye having equal seniority, McIntyre having greater seniority by reason of having qualified earlier.

Senator Young of Ohio, who faces a tough election campaign next year, had applied and was pressing the membership on the Finance Committee and had indicated that that was his first choice. He was, however, given his second choice, which was the Armed Services Committee, despite the fact that Senator Hart and Senator Moss, who had equal seniority, were also applicants for the position.

This, of course, is the kind of hard choice which faces members of the steering committee when they cannot be guided by seniority and there is not much by way of any other guide to turn to. Senators Moss and Hart also face difficult campaigns.

If, as then had become apparent, it was difficult to put Senator Young of Ohio on the Finance Committee, it certainly was entirely appropriate to put him on the Armed Services Committee. But consider what happened to the other vacancy. The other vacancy was filled, not by Senator Hart, not by Senator Moss, or by Senator McIntyre, but by Senator Inouye.

I suggest that on the basis of experience and on the basis of the needs of the other two Senators, the claims of Senators Hart and Moss were superior to those of Senator Inouye, who received a fine appointment to the Public Works Committee, a committee of great importance to the State of Hawaii, and who could well have been appointed to another major committee had it been decided to favor the application of either Senator Hart or Senator Moss.

So for the third time seniority was ignored in filling committee vacancies.

MR. MANSFIELD Mr. President, will the Senator yield?

MR. CLARK I am happy to yield.

MR. MANSFIELD Does the Senator recall that a couple of years ago when I went to him, after I had first become the leader, and said, "Joe, would you mind getting off one committee and getting on another one." He said, "No. I am fourth in seniority on this committee. I am accumulating seniority. I do not want to get off"?

MR. CLARK If the Senator says I said that, I will take his word for it.

MR. MANSFIELD It was only 2 years ago.

MR. CLARK If the Senator says so, I take his word. The Senator will also recall that I offered, without being asked to do so to get off a committee in order that other Senators might receive appointment to a certain committee.

MR. MANSFIELD The Senator is correct. I could go into further details, but I will not. I will merely say that the Senator is correct.

MR. CLARK I thank the Senator.

Now I turn to another "Orphan Annie," the Committee on Banking and Currency. What a shame that it is an "Orphan Annie," because it is one of the most important committees of the Senate. I suppose this is the committee the Senator from Montana was talking about a moment ago.

MR. MANSFIELD That is the one.

MR. CLARK Apparently my devotion to that committee is not shared by my colleagues, because there was only one applicant for that committee, and that applicant, Senator McIntyre, would have been an appropriate selection for other committees rather than that one. I welcome him as a member of the committee. I note the presence in the Chamber of the Senator from Illinois, the Senator from Wisconsin, and the Senator from New York. I think they will agree with me that that is a fine committee and that we all deplore the fact that other Senators do not want the assignment. So there was no controversy involving the Committee on Banking and Currency. One freshman Senator was willing to apply—

MR. LONG of Louisiana Mr. President, will the Senator yield?

MR. CLARK I yield.

MR. LONG of Louisiana I agree that the Banking and Currency Committee is a very good committee. This Senator gave up two committees to get on it when he was a freshman. He does not regret that action, because he thinks it was a fine opportunity to serve this body.

MR. CLARK I thank the Senator.

I turn now to the Commerce Committee, where the ratio was changed from 11 Democrats and 6 Republicans to 12 Democrats and 5 Republicans. I note that there were two vacancies and they eventually were filled on the basis of seniority, and Senator Hart joined Senator Cannon in filling the second vacancy, after the committee had preliminarily made another decision; and I will not go into that.

I point out the fortunate spot in which my friend the Senator from Nevada finds himself. He is now on Commerce, Space, Armed Services, and Rules. I admire—and I really do admire—the ability which he has displayed on the three committees on which he already serves, and it is true that he had seniority over the other applicants on Commerce. I have no criticism of what was done in that connection in the end.

The poor District of Columbia Committee comes next. Having served for 2 years on that committee I deplore the fact that no one wants to serve on it. I wish I could induce some of the younger Senators what a wonderful committee that committee is on which to serve. I am a former mayor of Philadelphia, and, goodness knows, the District of Columbia deserves better consideration from Congress than it gets. However, we had no applicant for the vacancy on that committee. Therefore Senator McIntyre was, to some extent, shanghaied to serve on that committee. I believe he served with distinction as mayor of Laconia, N. H., before he came to the Senate.

Now we come to the *pièce de résistance,* if I may borrow a French phrase, and that is the Finance Committee. Here the battle raged, with bloodshed on all sides. The present ratio on the Finance Committee is, to my way of thinking—and I suppose some of my friends would agree with me—inexcusable. It is 11 Democrats and 6 Republicans. It is less than even 2 to 1, when we have 67 percent of the Members of the Senate. It is not proposed to change that ratio.

MR. DOUGLAS   Mr. President, will the Senator yield?

MR. CLARK   I shall yield in a moment. Where is the program of the President of the United States going to get stalled? Where is it going to get delayed? Where was medicare bottled up last year? Where are the tax bill and the tax reform bill in jeopardy this year? It is in the Finance Committee.

MR. DOUGLAS   Mr. President, will the Senator yield?

MR. CLARK   I am happy to yield to the Senator from Illinois.

MR. DOUGLAS   As a member of the Finance Committee I believe I can testify that when conference committees are set up there usually are, to represent the Senate, three members who say they belong to the Democratic Party and two Republicans, with the result that the conference committee always votes with the Republicans, and we are presented—and I now want to show my knowledge of French—with a *fait accompli*. The Republican version always wins.

MR. CLARK   This bilingual debate perhaps impresses the country with the erudition of our Members.

MR. LONG of Louisiana   Mr. President, will the Senator yield?

MR. CLARK   I am glad to yield to the distinguished and able member of the Finance Committee, the ranking Democratic member after the chairman, the Senator from Louisiana.

MR. LONG of Louisiana   The junior Senator from Louisiana had some doubt that the Democrats should have agreed to a ratio of 11 to 6 on that committee. He expressed some doubts on that subject. However, he was very much opposed to expanding the size of the Finance Committee, feeling that, if need be, it would be better to offer an amendment on the floor than to vote through a favorable committee recommendation by virtue of having expanded the size of the committee.

The Senator says that medicare was killed in committee. It is my impression that the medicare bill lost on the floor of the Senate by a single vote. The Senator from Louisiana, as well as other Senators on that committee, southerners in the main, on whom, the Senator has indicated, the Kennedy administration cannot rely, have undertaken to indicate to the administration and to other Democrats that we would have no intention of having any proposal of the administration bottled up in that committee. We would propose that if a majority of the committee wanted to recommend something contrary to what the President was recommending, we would be happy to see that there would be an opportunity to assure that the matter would be voted upon on the floor. As far as this Senator is concerned —and I believe I speak for a majority of the committee—there are enough votes on the committee to see that a bill will be presented on the floor to which the medicare plan can be offered as an amendment. As a matter of fact, under Senate procedure, it is difficult for anyone to prevent a Senator who believed in a particular proposal from having the opportunity to offer it or the floor.

MR. CLARK   I have no quarrel with what the Senator has said. I make the point that the representation on the Finance Committee should properly represent the representation of Democrats and Republicans in the Senate, instead of representing, as it does today—and I think this is not an extravagant statement to make—the well-known conservative bipartisan coalition opposed to the President of the United States.

MR. LONG of Louisiana   Mr. President, will the Senator yield?

MR. CLARK   I will yield in a minute. My point is that in connection with the committee a ratio of 14 to 7—with 21 members on the committee—14 Democrats and 7 Republicans would more justly and properly represent the membership in the Senate, because then supporters of the President and liberal Republicans could be placed on the committee, and we would have a situation where that committee would no longer be the principal deterrent to the President's program, where we would have a real chance of democratizing the Senate, where perhaps a new majority would increase the staff, and where on the basis of the new majority subcommittees would be appointed with real power to act, and where the proposed new ratio would make it possible to bring bills out of committee after 2 or 3 months of hearings instead of after 7 or 8 months of hearings.

I see my good friend the majority leader on his feet, and I believe that this is what he wanted to do also. Here is where we get bipartisan. The reason we are not going to increase the size of the Finance Committee is because a fairly careful and accurate nose count revealed that we could not get even one Republican vote to make that committee represent the proper representation in the Senate.

MR. JAVITS Mr. President, will the Senator yield?

MR. CLARK We were told it would be necessary to get all of the votes to change the size of that committee. On the Democratic side, we have 67 Senators. We knew there would be 20 Senators who would not vote with us. That leaves 47. We were told there were 33 solid Republican votes against increasing the size of the committee.

MR. MANSFIELD and MR. JAVITS addressed the Chair.

The PRESIDING OFFICER Does the Senator from Pennsylvania yield; and, if so, to whom does he yield?

MR. CLARK I yield first to the majority leader; and then to the Senator from New York.

MR. MANSFIELD I really dislike to wash our dirty Democratic linen in public, but I suppose it has to be done once in a while.

MR. CLARK The Senator will recall that I urged him at the steering committee meeting to allow us to review these matters in the Democratic conference. For reasons I understand and with which I can even sympathize, he said that he would rather have it done on the floor.

MR. MANSFIELD That still does not change my mind.

MR. CLARK I did not think it would.

MR. MANSFIELD I still dislike it. However, I should like to say that there has been some talk in the press that the Senator from Montana, acting as majority leader, was some sort of martyr in assuming the blame for trying to bring about an increase in the Finance Committee. I am no martyr. I never have been. I do not believe I would qualify to be a martyr.

MR. CLARK If the Senator will permit an interjection, I would like to say that he is the closest to any martyr that I have ever seen on the floor of the Senate, and I honor him for it.

MR. MANSFIELD I thank the Senator. Let me say this, however. A few months ago I received a letter from the Senator from Pennsylvania [Mr. Clark] who now controls the floor, at which time he made the suggestion that because of the increase in the

Democratic membership in the Senate, the ratio in the Finance Committee should be changed in proportion.

I thought it was a good idea. I called it to the attention of the President. He said, "That is your business; it is the Senate's business." He indicated that he was interested in the tax bill, but so far as the ratio of membership on the committee was concerned, he showed no interest.

But I wish to give credit where credit is due. The Senator from Pennsylvania [Mr. Clark] originated the idea. I picked it up— I tried to sell it. I did not get much response.

The problem comes down to a matter of political arithmetic. Certain members of the Committee on Finance—not the chairman of the committee—and other Senators came to me and said, "We do not want the membership of the Committee on Finance to be increased." I was told by the other side that there would be 33 solid votes against an increase in the membership of the committee.

MR. CLARK Mr. President, will the Senator from Montana yield?

MR. MANSFIELD I yield.

MR. CLARK My understanding is that that information came when the discussed increase was to be in a ratio of 13 to 6, not, as I have suggested, 14 to 7, which would have enabled still another Republican Senator, other than the minority leader, to become a member of the committee.

MR. MANSFIELD The Senator is correct. I think it is a part of my job on occasion to take a poll on the Democratic side. I asked the assistant majority leader, the Senator from Minnesota [Mr. Humphrey], and the secretary for the majority to conduct a quiet poll. I say to the Senator from Pennsylvania that on the basis of that poll, we would have got, at the very most, between 40 and 42 votes.

MR. CLARK All Democratic.

MR. MANSFIELD All Democratic. It was merely a case of simple arithmetic.

From time to time I have heard that the distinguished Senator from Virginia [Mr. Byrd], the chairman of the Committee on Finance, has indicated his opposition to what some refer jokingly as the packing of the Committee on Finance. To the best of my knowledge, the Senator from Virginia, who is a very fair-minded man, never took a position, never said a word, although I was quite sure in my own mind that he would be against such a proposal.

I may say also—and I am glad that the Senator from Illinois [Mr. Douglas] is in the Chamber—that, to the best of my knowledge, the Senator from Virginia has not held up proposed legislation in the Committee on Finance, even though he was opposed to it. He has always allowed measures to come to the floor of the Senate. I have tried to get him to speed up matters, as I did 2 years ago, asking if it would not be possible for the chairman of the House Committee on Ways and Means and the chairman of the Committee on Finance to hold hearings simultaneously on tax bills. They both put me in my place in a hurry, saying that they would not do that, but would follow the customary procedure.

All too often in this body a Senator is crucified or pilloried because he is supposed to have indicated his position about this or that subject or his support of this or that measure. As we operate in this Chamber, we may not like the views of our colleagues, but we come to know them and appreciate their honesty. I apply that statement to every Member of this body.

MR. CLARK The Senator is correct. I have no quarrel with his statement.

I yield now to the Senator from Illinois, so that he may ask a question of the Senator from Montana.

MR. DOUGLAS I do not wish to ask a question of the Senator from Montana; but since the Senator from Montana pointed me out as being in the Chamber, I thought I should make it clear that I have never accused the Senator from Virginia of holding up proposed legislation. At times, I think hearings before the Finance Committee are prolonged, but I have never accused the Senator from Virginia of preventing proposed legislation from coming to the floor of the Senate.

If there was unintentionally on the part of the Senator from Montana the imputation that I had made such a charge, I hope the Senator from Montana will withdraw it.

MR. MANSFIELD   Mr. President, will the Senator from Pennsylvania yield?

MR. CLARK   I yield.

MR. MANSFIELD   If there was an imputation of that nature, I, of course, withdraw it. I called the attention of the Senate to the Senator from Illinois because, so far as I could see, he was the only member of the Committee on Finance who was present in the Chamber. Now I observe that the Senator from Louisiana [Mr. Long] also is in the Chamber. I thought the Senator from Illinois would either corroborate or disprove what I said, because I was making a statement which was subject to correction, and I was looking to the Senator from Illinois for guidance one way or the other.

MR. DOUGLAS   Have I supplied that guidance now?

MR. MANSFIELD   The Senator has.

MR. DOUGLAS   I thank the Senator.

MR. MANSFIELD   If the Senator from Pennsylvania will further yield, I think I have said about all I wanted to say. I wanted the *Record* to show that the baby—the idea of increasing the membership of the Committee on Finance—had as its proud father the Senator from Pennsylvania [Mr. Clark]; that the Senator from Montana took up the idea and tried to sell it, but did not get very far with it; but just before the steering committee met, had a quiet poll taken, and learned that the necessary votes were not available; he then went to the steering committee and recommended that there be no change. I want the *Record* to be clear.

MR. CLARK   I thank the Senator from Montana, whose statement of the facts, as I understand them, is completely accurate.

While no doubt it is true that the White House did not inject itself in such fashion as to apply pressure concerning the size of the Committee on Finance, I suspect that those who know the President of the United States would not be far off if we felt that he would not have been seriously disappointed if he found that the size of the Committee on Finance had been increased or a more favorable Democratic ratio achieved.

Mr. President, I am about to conclude, and shall therefore willingly yield the floor in a few minutes. It will not be "senatorial" minutes; it will be time minutes.

I yield to the Senator from New York.

MR. JAVITS   Mr. President, I heard the Senator from Pennsylvania say something about 33 solid Republican votes. I am only one Republican, but I have no commitment with respect to being opposed to an increase in the membership of the Finance Committee.

We heard our southern friends argue—most sincerely, I am sure—that the number of Senators whose names appear on a bill does not mean that they are going to vote in favor of the bill. We saw an example of that in connection with the so-called Bricker amendment, which had as its sponsors an overwhelming majority of the Senate, yet failed of passage.

So I hope that whatever the Senator from Pennsylvania may have in mind today in terms of his point of view and his principles, and what he believes to be in the interest of the Senate and of the country, he will not be bedazzled by numbers. I knew nothing about the necessity of 33. I am sure those who made the statement made it in complete good faith. But I should like to have the Senator know that I am one Republican Senator who is not in the least committed as to how he will vote on any motion or resolution with respect to the composition of a committee.

MR. CLARK   I am cheered and heartened by the sentiments of the Senator from New York.

Mr. President, I observe in the Chamber several other Senators who I know wish to speak before the Senate adjourns. I shall complete my speech in a few minutes. I desire to speak a further word about the Committee on Finance. Then I shall yield to Senators who wish me to yield to them. I desire to submit some motions, but first I wish to conclude my remarks about the Committee on Finance.

Having determined not to change the ratio of membership on the Committee on Finance for the reasons stated by the majority leader, we were confronted with one vacancy on the committee. In the order of original seniority, the applicants for that position were: Senator Proxmire, Senator Young of Ohio, Senator Cannon, and Senator Long of Missouri. A last-minute added starter was the senior Senator from Ohio [Mr. Lausche], who was the senior of them all, so far as this list is concerned. But all those Senators—Senator Lausche, Senator Proxmire, Senator Young of Ohio, Senator Cannon, and Senator Long of Missouri —were bypassed. Seniority was ignored again, and my very dear friend the able Senator from Connecticut, the distinguished former Secretary of Health, Education, and Welfare [Mr. Ribicoff], a man having a brilliant political record, was pushed ahead of all the other Senators and placed on the Committee on Finance.

At this point, I shall discontinue my seriatim discussion of the actions of the steering committee and I shall resume what I have to say about it tomorrow, when the opportunity presents itself. I shall yield in a moment to the Senator from Illinois and the Senator from Wisconsin, who would like to have me yield to them; but before doing so, I send to the desk, in accordance with rule XL, of the Standing Rules of the Senate, three written notices of motions to amend rule XXV and three resolutions to amend rule XXV. I ask that the resolutions be printed and lie at the desk.

The PRESIDING OFFICER   The notices of motions to suspend the rule will be received, printed, printed in the *Record,* and will lie on the desk.

The notices and resolutions are as follows:

NOTICE OF MOTION TO AMEND RULE XXV

In accordance with rule XL of the Standing Rules of the Senate, I hereby give notice in writing that it is my intention to move to amend rule XXV, as follows:

"*Resolved,* That rule XXV of the Standing Rules of the Senate be amended as follows:

"In paragraph (b) (dealing with the Committee on Appropriations) of subsection 1 of rule XXV, strike out the word 'twenty-seven' and insert in lieu thereof 'twenty-nine'."

The purpose of the proposed amendment is to increase the size of the Committee on Appropriations by 2 seats to 29.

NOTICE OF MOTION TO AMEND RULE XXV

In accordance with rule XL of the Standing Rules of the Senate, I hereby give notice in writing that it is my intention to move to amend rule XXV, as follows:

"*Resolved,* That rule XXV of the standing Rules of the Senate be amended as follows:

"In paragraph (h) (dealing with the Committee on Finance) of subsection 1 of rule XXV, strike out the word 'seventeen' and insert in lieu thereof 'twenty-one'."

The purpose of the proposed amendment is to increase the size of the Committee on Finance by 4 seats to 21.

NOTICE OF MOTION TO AMEND RULE XXV

In accordance with rule XL of the Standing Rules of the Senate, I hereby give notice in writing that it is my intention to move to amend rule XXV, as follows:

"*Resolved*, That rule XXV of the Standing Rules of the Senate be amended as follows:

"In paragraph (i) (dealing with the Committee on Foreign Relations) of subsection 1 of rule XXV, strike out the word 'seventeen' and insert in lieu thereof 'twenty-one'."

The purpose of the proposed amendment is to increase the size of the Committee on Foreign Relations by 4 seats to 21.

S. RES. 91

Resolved, That rule XXV of the Standing Rules of the Senate be amended as follows:

In paragraph (b) (dealing with the Committee on Appropriations) of subsection 1 of rule XXV, strike out the word "twenty-seven" and insert in lieu thereof "twenty-nine".

S. RES. 92

Resolved, That rule XXV of the Standing Rules of the Senate be amended as follows:

In paragraph (i) (dealing with the Committee on Foreign Relations) of subsection 1 of rule XXV, strike out the word "seventeen" and insert in lieu thereof "twenty-one".

S. RES. 93

Resolved, That rule XXV of the Standing Rules of the Senate be amended as follows:

In paragraph (h) (dealing with the Committee on Finance) of subsection 1 of the rule XXV, strike out the word "seventeen" and insert in lieu thereof "twenty-one".

MR. CLARK   Mr. President, the motions and resolutions would increase the size of the Committee on Appropriations by two; would increase the size of the Committee on Finance by four; and would increase the size of the Committee on Foreign Relations by four. I shall speak tomorrow about why it seems to me these proposed changes in rule XXV are in the public interest.

I shall yield first to the distinguished Senator from Illinois and then to the distinguished Senator from Wisconsin.

MR. DOUGLAS   Mr. President, I have followed with great interest this very detailed analysis by the Senator from Pennsylvania and wish to commend him for it. I think I should make a public explanation as to why I was not present at the meeting of the steering committee.

MR. CLARK   Mr. President, will the Senator from Illinois permit me to interrupt him?

MR. DOUGLAS   I yield.

MR. CLARK   The proxy of the Senator from Illinois was voted on all these matters, as were the proxies of at least two other Senators, distinguished Members of the establishment, who were not at the meeting either.

MR. DOUGLAS   In December, I wrote to the whip of the Democratic group saying that I assumed that, as usual, the Republicans would "take off" between February 8 and 19 to praise the memory of Abraham Lincoln—

MR. CLARK   Having just voted by a substantial majority to ignore the 13th and 14th amendments.

MR. DOUGLAS   Yes; and that the Senate would oblige our Republican friends by closing down and transacting no business. It seemed to me that if that was to be done, I would have the right to go to Illinois in order to prove that Abraham Lincoln was a spiritual Democrat. I asked the whip to inform me whether I would cripple the work of the Senate if I absented myself during this period when our Republican friends were to be absent. I received no such warning from him. I asked him verbally whether the Senate would be in the doldrums during this time. I was informed that it would be. So I made my plans to spend 10 days in Illinois, and to deliver approximately 40 speeches.

I went to the Democratic conference on Thursday, the 7th; and on the secret ballot I voted with the Senator from Pennsylvania [Mr. Clark] to enlarge the steering committee to 19; but when a secret ballot was objected to, I voted—on the motion of the Senator from New Mexico—to increase the membership to 17.

But then I had to return to my office, to pack my bag, so as to be ready to go back to Illinois. Just as I was about to leave,

I found—to my surprise—that I had been designated a member of the steering committee—something which I had not anticipated would happen.

MR. CLARK Although the Senator from Illinois was a candidate for it, was he not?

MR. DOUGLAS Yes.

MR. MANSFIELD Mr. President, will the Senator from Pennsylvania yield?

MR. CLARK I yield.

MR. MANSFIELD I believe the Senator from Illinois was given a choice—namely, assignment to either the steering committee or the policy committee. Is that correct?

MR. DOUGLAS That is correct.

MR. MANSFIELD And the assistant majority leader and I thought the Senator from Illinois would be more interested in becoming a member of the policy committee. However, his choice was assignment to the steering committee, and he received that assignment.

MR. DOUGLAS That is correct.

MR. MANSFIELD Let me say that during the period in which I have been the leader on this side, there have been only four vacancies in the membership of that committee, and those have been filled by the Senator from Pennsylvania [Mr. Clark], the Senator from Illinois [Mr. Douglas], the Senator from New Jersey [Mr. Williams], and the Senator from Connecticut [Mr. Dodd].

MR. DOUGLAS I could not be present at the time when action was taken in regard to the membership of that committee because of necessary preparations prior to my scheduled departure to Illinois. If I had known in advance that that action would be taken, I would have canceled my other engagements. But having made them, I could not cancel them then. So I gave my proxy to the Senator from Pennsylvania, with certain instructions— except that as to one committee assignment, to which he was an aspirant, I felt that it would not be proper for me to give my proxy to him. So I gave it to another Senator, with instructions to vote for the Senator from Pennsylvania.

I say this only in explanation of why I was absent; and I

make this statement only in view of the fact that it has been bruited about that I cared so little about what would happen that I did not attend the committee meeting.

Now, in connection with the detailed explanation which the Senator from Pennsylvania is giving today, and which I understand he will continue tomorrow, let me say that as I examine the committee assignments I am compelled to ask whether a certain pattern seems to emerge—namely, that seniority is disregarded in a significant number of cases of Senators who vote to restrict the filibuster and to apply a more rigid cloture rule, and that such Senators are passed over, in favor of Senators who vote to maintain the filibuster and to oppose more stringent cloture. Am I correct in this?

MR. MANSFIELD   Mr. President, as to that, let me say that I think—

MR. CLARK   Mr. President, if I may, I should like to answer the question.

MR. MANSFIELD   Very well.

MR. CLARK   I do not make that charge.

MR. MANSFIELD   And the charge is not true.

MR. DOUGLAS   I do not make the charge. I simply ask whether this pattern emerges. It seemed to me that it did.

MR. MANSFIELD   No; it does not.

Mr. President, will the Senator from Pennsylvania yield?

MR. CLARK   I yield.

MR. MANSFIELD   What was the position of the Senator from Indiana [Mr. Bayh] on the filibuster and also the position of Senators Brewster, Edmondson, Inouye, Kennedy, McGovern, McIntyre, Nelson, and Ribicoff? I think they were 7 to 2 against the filibuster. However, all but two of these Senators received both committee assignments they requested; and the other two received one-half of their requested committee assignments.

MR. DOUGLAS   I do not wish to go into that matter. But, as I recall, the Senator from Hawaii [Mr. Inouye] voted to maintain the present filibuster rule.

MR. MANSFIELD   That is correct; the Senator from Hawaii [Mr. Inouye] and Senator—

MR. DOUGLAS   And a number of other new Senators were placed on the committees, ahead of Senators who have seniority.

MR. MANSFIELD   The Senator from Illinois is correct.

However, it was charged that, on the basis of these committee assignments, a "pattern" which "developed" indicated that those who were favored evidently voted for the filibuster, and that those who were not favored voted against the filibuster. But seven of the freshman Senators voted against the filibuster, and they were not punished in any way, nor were they favored; all of them were given equal consideration.

So far as the other Members are concerned—myself, the Senator from Alaska [Mr. Bartlett], the Senator from Ohio [Mr. Young], the Senator from Nevada [Mr. Cannon], the Senator from Michigan [Mr. Hart], the Senator from Florida [Mr. Smathers], the Senator from Rhode Island [Mr. Pell], the Senator from Arizona [Mr. Hayden], the Senator from Wyoming [Mr. McGee], the Senator from North Carolina [Mr. Jordan], the Senator from West Virginia [Mr. Byrd], and the Senator from Pennsylvania [Mr. Clark]—of that number, seven were for filibusters, as I interpret that, and five were against. So I would say that, if anything, the assignments were weighted on the other side.

Therefore, I do not like to have any Senator allege on this floor that a "pattern" was "developing," and that it indicated that the steering committee is favoring or punishing Senators.

Let me say, as one who has been charged with "indecisive leadership," that if Senators want a steering committee to function, they had better give it responsibility. If Senators do not want a steering committee to function, they should vote to abolish it, and to let the majority leader make the recommendations. So Senators should make that choice.

MR. PROXMIRE   Mr. President—

MR. CLARK   Mr. President, I yield now to the Senator from Wisconsin, unless the Senator from Illinois desires to have me yield further to him.

MR. DOUGLAS   Well, Mr. President, it is always ungracious to go into great detail in connection with these matters. I merely think that if an analysis is made of the record which the Senator from Pennsylvania is now establishing, and which he undoubtedly will establish in greater detail tomorrow, it will be found that it presents the very interesting question of whether such a pattern does develop; at least in the case of the "second generation" Senators, and it would be very interesting for the political analysts to go into this matter in some detail.

MR. MANSFIELD Mr. President, will the Senator from Pennsylvania yield?

MR. CLARK I yield.

MR. MANSFIELD Again the Senator from Illinois is raising the question of "a pattern." Let me say most sincerely and respectfully that I hope the Senator from Pennsylvania, who has gone very thoroughly into the subject—perhaps more thoroughly than any other Senator—will answer that allegation, and will do so now, and will do so on the basis of his knowledge and on the basis of the record to which he has access.

MR. CLARK Well, Mr. President, the majority leader makes a request which I find a very difficult one. A moment ago I said I do not charge that there is such a pattern—nor do I charge it now.

MR. MANSFIELD Yes.

MR. CLARK I think I would rather leave the matter this way: That overnight I will give some thought to the request of the Senator from Montana; and before I yield the floor tomorrow, I will answer his question, after some further analysis of the facts and figures.

MR. MANSFIELD I am delighted about that, because it is sufficiently difficult just to be a Democrat, with the divergencies which exist in our party. So I hope that instead of splitting ourselves apart, we shall do all we can to bring ourselves together.

That is something which is not my responsibility. It is not the responsibility of any individual Senator, but is the responsibility of all Senators.

MR. CLARK I yield to the Senator from Wisconsin.

MR. PROXMIRE Mr. President, the distinguished Senator from Pennsylvania, as is typical of him, has had the courage and conviction to make a very difficult speech. It is a speech that most Senators would not make. It was a speech in which he challenged the power and influence of those who control the U.S. Senate.

The Senator from Pennsylvania cannot possibly obtain any personal gain from his speech.

MR. CLARK   That is very clear.

MR. PROXMIRE   That is a masterpiece of understatement.

MR. CLARK   Yes; it is a masterpiece of understatement.

MR. MANSFIELD   I may say that I get no personal pleasure from it, either.

MR. PROXMIRE   Mr. President, our distinguished majority leader, the Senator from Montana, has done a marvelous job as majority leader. No one serving as chairman of the steering committee could have done a better job.

However, I shall make a suggestion in a constructive way as to how I hope the kind of serious problem raised by the Senator from Pennsylvania can be solved.

We invariably follow a seniority principle in selecting the chairmen of Senate committees. That is certainly one of the most important assignments a Senator can get. A chairman of a standing committee is in a powerful position in this body. Invariably we follow the seniority principle in appointing Senators as chairmen of subcommittees; or at least invariably every Senator has an opportunity, if he wishes to become chairman of a subcommittee, to become such in order of seniority.

One recognized exception has been made in making committee appointments under the seniority rule. Everyone I know in the Democratic Party approves. That is that newly elected Senators are appointed to committees regardless of their seniority position. That is the only way in which Senators from two-party States would have an opportunity to serve on powerful committees. That is good.

MR. CLARK   Mr. President, will the Senator yield?

MR. PROXMIRE   I shall yield in a moment. I should like to finish my thought. While we should place trust in the steering committee—and I want to do so—I can see no reason on earth why we should not provide that, with the exception of the appointment of junior or newly elected Senators—

MR. CLARK   To one committee.

MR. PROXMIRE   To one committee, or we can modify it in any way we wish—but the point I wish to make today is that, with the exception of the assignment of new Senators, seniority should be followed religiously in making other appointments to committees. There is a strong case against the seniority principle.

Frankly, if we could eliminate seniority in toto from committee assignments, I would vote to do so. But we cannot do this. We will not do it.

Seniority in committee assignments is a way of life. If we are realistic we accept it. We live with it. But then we should apply it with scrupulous fairness, with no partiality, with no favor.

This is not the case now, and every Senator knows it.

If we do not follow this principle in all cases and without partiality, I submit to my good friend from Illinois [Mr. Douglas] and to my good friend the Senator from Pennsylvania [Mr. Clark], that whether we like it or not, we shall be at the mercy of the steering committee, and some of us, rightly or wrongly, feel that the steering committee may have bias. I am not saying that individual Senators are not men of highest principle, but all of us have biases. One Senator may feel that the Senator from Alaska who won the appropriations assignment over the Senator from Texas, although the Senator from Texas is senior to the Senator from Alaska, is better qualified, others may feel that the Senator from Texas is better qualified than the Senator from Alaska. But who is better qualified? We can never decide that question. What makes a qualified Senator? Diligence, intelligence, eloquence, force, judgment? These are all largely subjective qualities. I suppose there may be some objective measurement of diligence, but we can never establish it, and no one tries to establish it in making committee assignments.

The fact is that appointments to committees are not based upon seniority. In several cases cited by the Senator from Pennsylvania they violated seniority although new Members were not involved. What were these assignments based on? Ideological favoritism? Favoritism based upon personal friendship? Of course they were. And if we are honest we will admit it. But neither of these considerations should have any bearing.

Therefore, I submit that it would be far easier for the steering committee if it followed seniority principle without favor or discrimination. There would not be this kind of dispute we have had this afternoon which is bound to develop in future years, which is bound to erode our confidence in each other, and which is bound to split our party. If straight seniority, except for newly elected Members, were the rule, I would not have been appointed to the Committee on Appropriations. The Senator from Texas [Mr. Yarborough] would have been appointed. The Senator from Connecticut [Mr. Ribicoff] would have been appointed to the Committee on Finance. He is a newly elected Senator and, under the rule, entitled to one major committee assignment.

At the same time, I feel that if we Democratic Senators do not insist on some kind of seniority rule, we should accept the action taken by the steering committee. We have no one to blame but ourselves. The steering committee is outnumbered in the caucus. And any time we wish to do so, we Democratic Senators can insist on the seniority rule being applied without favor. I think we ought to do it. The speech of the Senator from Pennsylvania was an excellent speech. It was well documented. It was in excellent taste. No one should have been offended by it. As I said, it is difficult to make a speech of that kind. In this Senator's judgment it was a conclusive argument for the application of straight seniority from now on.

MR. CLARK   Mr. President, with deep regret I find myself unable to agree in full.

MR. PROXMIRE   That is the trouble with us liberals. We can never get together.

MR. CLARK   I will try to develop the question of the seniority rule further tomorrow before this matter is concluded.

Unless some other Senator present in the Chamber desires to ask me a question or to engage in colloquy, I should like to yield the floor.

MR. MANSFIELD   Mr. President, will the Senator yield?

MR. CLARK   I yield to the Senator from Montana.

MR. MANSFIELD   Much as I disagree with a great deal of what the Senator from Pennsylvania has said this afternoon, I commend him and compliment him for the dignified way in which he has presented his subject. I agree with the Senator from Wisconsin that it was not a pleasant duty. I am sure the Senator looks upon it as a duty. From his point of view, he thinks it should be done. That is all right. But I express the hope that what has taken place will not become an annual ritual. I hope that we shall try, as much as possible, to do away with these differences between Democrats, and look upon ourselves not as liberals, conservatives, or middle-of-the-roaders, but as a part of the Democratic Party and as Democrats. We have our differences, but perhaps we can obviate them. Again I wish to compliment the Senator for the dignified way in which he presented his case today.

MR. CLARK   I thank my friend for his very kind words. Coming from him at this time of the day, they are doubly appreciated because I know the speech I have just made must have been in many ways disheartening to the majority leader. His reaction to it is typical of the generous and gentlemanly way in which he treats all Senators, regardless of which side of the aisle they may be on.

The best way I can think of to avoid this semiannual ritual is to reorganize the steering committee so that it properly represents the Democratic majority in the U.S. Senate.

MR. MOSS   Mr. President, will the Senator yield?

MR. CLARK   I am happy to yield to the distinguished Senator from Utah.

MR. MOSS   I commend the Senator from Pennsylvania for the very detailed, thoughtful, and restrained speech that he has delivered. It is indeed a difficult subject. I have refrained from taking any part in the discussion because personal involvement on my part is great. But I have listened with the greatest of interest.

I feel that the problem that has been discussed here by the senior Senator from Pennsylvania is one of such great importance that it should have been aired on the floor of the Senate, and it should be in the permanent *Record* of the Senate as a discussion. I, like other Democrats, regret when there is disagreement among Democrats. But the only way I know to straighten it out is to have a full and frank discussion of the problem and some recommended remedies, and then proceed in some democratic way to achieve the desired result. I appreciate very much the

Senator's undertaking to do what he has done, because I felt many Senators who were involved as a part of the problem could not discuss it objectively. I think the Senator has undertaken to discuss the problem in an objective and intellectual manner.

MR. CLARK   I thank my friend from Utah for his kind words. I express the hope that sometime between now and November 1964, the Senator from Utah will obtain one of the committee assignments he so assiduously seeks and to which he is so justly entitled.

MR. MORSE   Mr. President, will the Senator yield?

MR. CLARK   I yield.

MR. MORSE   I shall obtain the floor in my own right later to speak on another subject, but I wish to comment on the debate that has taken place this afternoon. I am not speaking in agreement in the Senate except with seven other Senators. But if the debate has proved anything today, in my judgment it has proved the soundness of the position of those of us in the Democratic caucus who supported my motion that the steering committee should be checked according to the good old Jeffersonian philosophical democratic principle.

Basic in the philosophy of Jefferson was the principle of checks and balances. He knew that power given to mere men would be abused unless checked. He knew that government by law cannot exist unless the mere men who administer government are checked in the exercise of their power.

If the steering committee were subject to the motion I made in the Democratic Party conference it would have been checked by requiring it to submit its decisions on committee appointments to the entire Democratic conference membership for a check. The power of finality to make committee assignments should be checked by the requirement my motion proposed. Eight of us, Douglas, Clark, Neuberger, McNamara, Proxmire, Nelson, Gruening, and Morse supported this elementary and fundamental principle of Jeffersonian democracy. It is my hope that this debate this afternoon has proven to a majority of my colleagues that in 1964 the amendment I offered to check the steering committee will be adopted.

I do not know of anything that could have proved the soundness of that motion more than the debate on the floor of the Senate this afternoon. As I just stated, I hope that between now and 1964 that rollcall of eight who supported the Morse motion will increase to a majority, because that is the place to iron out party difficulties. Had we had that conference, in my judgment the report of the steering committee this year would have been modified after debate and conference.

I speak as one who probably bears more battle scars over committee fights in the past 18 years than any other Member of this body. Although I am a Member on this side of the aisle, I shall never forget the 19-to-19 vote tie in 1953 which was cast here in the Senate, which was finally broken by our then majority leader with his own vote, in order to subject the Senator from Oregon to Republican discipline.

At that time my right to continue on the committees on which I had been serving for years was destroyed by partisan politics in the Senate. As I said then the sovereign State of Oregon was wronged by a partisan arrangement which relegated me to the Republicans for discipline on committee assignments because I exercised an honest independence of judgment in resigning from the Republican Party. I have no regrets for my course of action because the sorry record of the Republican Party before and since justified my decision. However, the Senate wrote a sorry record in that committee fight because it did irreparable damage not to the Senator from Oregon but to the seniority system in the Senate. Many a Senator since then has told me that he made a great mistake in yielding to the partisanship of the hour.

I felt then that we ought to recognize the importance of improving the procedure of the Senate in connection with the assignments to committees. The debate this afternoon, I think, has proved my case.

I rest my case.

MR. CLARK Mr. President, I thank the Senator from Oregon for his kind comments. I point out that I was one of the eight who joined the Senator in the rather hopeless fight to have the Democratic conference approve the selections of the steering committee.

Mr. President, I yield the floor.

MR. JAVITS   Mr. President, the matter of my place upon the Appropriations Committee has been discussed twice today. One of those discussions related to the views of the Senator from Georgia about certain speculation in the press on the reasons for this action on the part of the majority party. The other analyzed the internal procedures of the Democratic Party. In both discussions I think one thing has not been made clear.

I have already expressed my personal feeling. As the person concerned, I have preferred to regard this whole unfortunate development as one of the vicissitudes of politics in the field in which we are engaged. Those who wish to speculate, of course, have every right to do so on their own; but, the central point which I should like to make before this part of the debate concludes is that clearly some other course could have been taken instead of displacing a Senator who is already a member of the Appropriations Committee.

What is very important is the case of New York. New York has not had sufficient representation on the Appropriations Committee. There have been only five New Yorkers on the committee in the whole history of the Senate.

The position of New York in the Nation as a critically important center of commerce and finance is well recognized. Whatever may be said about the contributions of other States to the central position of New York—and no one is quicker to acknowledge those contributions than I—the fact is that New York is the financial center of the country. It has been so because of the acumen, the skill, the hard work, the diligence and the traditional position of our banks and financial institutions, of our trades industries—service and otherwise—of our technicians, architects, and engineers, the whole range of magnificent service which is available to this country in New York.

In view of these facts, it is strangely anomalous that when, finally, a Member from New York is placed on the Appropriations Committee, this unfortunate problem of displacement occurs.

So, Mr. President, I must report to the Senate that in New York there is a very strong feeling that the people of the State of New York deserve some explanation. An effort is being made to give it here on the floor. The people of New York deserve to have the questions answered, as to whether this was arbitrary, as to whether it was purposeful, or not.

It is in that sense and only in that sense that I speak, Mr. President. Therefore, I think that, quite apart from the critical importance of reforming whatever processes need reform, and quite apart from the desire of Members to set the record straight so far as they are concerned, the present debate will be illuminating to the people of New York as to how and why this event occurred in quite the fashion that it did.

Mr. President, I repeat what I said this morning. Personally, I take this reverse philosophically. However, I think the people of my State must be informed. I will continue to do my utmost to serve the people of my State on the committees on which I sit, as well as on the floor of the Senate.

MR. KEATING   Mr. President, will the Senator yield to me?

MR. JAVITS   I yield.

MR. KEATING   I shall not mention, Mr. President, any reference to the reasons for the action which was taken. I want my colleague to know that I share with him regret over the action. It is my feeling that New York needs a member on the Appropriations Committee. I have complete confidence in the work of my distinguished colleague. I express to him my personal appreciation, as well as the appreciation of the people of New York, for the service which he has rendered on the committee, which, in my judgment, is deserving of his continuance on the committee.

I regret very deeply, both for myself and for the people of the State of New York, the action which has been taken, which has deprived my colleague of the place on the committee on which he was serving with such outstanding distinction.

February 20, 1963

MR. CLARK Mr. President, I resume my discussion of the Senate establishment which I began yesterday. I shall probably not conclude this afternoon, owing to the lateness of the hour at which I have obtained the floor and my desire not to hold the Senate unduly late in session; but I shall speak, if other Senators are interested in the timing, for probably about an hour. If there are Senators present who wish me to yield to them to make brief remarks, I shall be glad to do so at any time.

FINANCE COMMITTEE

Mr. President, when I concluded yesterday I was discussing the impact of the bipartisan Senate establishment on the composition and size of the Senate Finance Committee. I pointed out that for various reasons, which I discussed yesterday in a speech which concluded in the *Record* for yesterday in the first column of page 2423, it had been determined by the Senate establishment, and the majority leader felt that the establishment in this instance had the votes, to retain the size of the Finance Committee at 17 members, and to divide those 17 between Republicans and Democrats in the ratio of 11 Democrats to 6 Republicans, even though there are 67 Democrats and only 33 Republicans in the Senate, which would justify a 12-to-5 ratio on the committee.

So that, in terms of that justice and equity which governed the ratio between Democrats and Republicans in assignments to practically every other committee, the ratio would be at least 14 to 7 or 10 to 5, and might conceivably be 13 to 6 or 12 to 5. Nevertheless, the establishment concluded to permit the bipartisan establishment control to continue without dilution in this important committee to which so large a share of the measures which the President of the United States believes important to the success of his program either have been or will be referred.

I pointed out also that the method in which the Finance Committee operates, and has operated for years, makes for long delay in reporting important measures to the floor of the Senate. Senators will recall how long it took before we were able to bring to a vote on the floor of the Senate the medicare bill, both last year and 2 years ago.

Senators will recall that there was no possibility of that bill's coming out of the Finance Committee in anything like the shape in which it was recommended by the President.

Senators will recall also that this year we have already been advised by the chairman of the Finance Committee that he sees no possibility of bringing a tax bill to the floor until after Labor Day.

The principal reason for this, to my way of thinking, untoward delay in enabling the program of the President to be voted on the floor of the Senate is threefold:

First, the Finance Committee is unwilling to conduct even preliminary hearings on the vitally important bills until the House has acted, although it had no hesitation in doing it with respect to the Du Pont bill recently, which the establishment favored.

It appears that when the program of the President is involved, the policy is one of "let's take our time." When a bill in which the establishment is interested is involved, the cue is, "Let's act with expedition."

The second reason is that, unlike almost any other committee in the Senate, the Finance Committee does not organize itself into subcommittees, so that all testimony is taken and the executive consideration of all bills is conducted before the entire committee, despite the fact that the Finance Committee has perhaps the most extended and complicated jurisdiction of any of the committees in the Senate.

For example, would it not be simple right now to divide the Finance Committee, let us say, into no more than two subcommittees? Let one of them conduct hearings on social security matters, such as medicare, while the other one is conducting hearings on the tax program of the President. In this way the business of the Senate would be enormously expedited, and it might even be possible to adjourn and go home before Labor Day.

I understand that other Senators may have under consideration a Senate resolution expressing the sense of the Senate that the Finance Committee should promptly begin hearings on the tax bill, and perhaps on the medicare bill, and be prepared to bring the tax bill to the floor of the Senate within 30 days of the time that the House acts, now thought to be the end of June.

I hope that these arguments will prevail on the minds of the majority of the members of the Finance Committee and that this type of expeditious action will take place.

The third reason why matters are so delayed in the Finance Committee is quite frankly and candidly because it has not an adequate staff in terms of the numbers of qualified men and women able to sift and analyze and report to the members of the committee on the complex tax structure and other matters, including social security and trade matters, which come before the committee, besides advising other Members of the Senate who may feel impelled by reason of an interest in the subject matter to seek the advice of members of the staff of the Finance Committee.

This void is filled only partially by the Joint Committee on Internal Revenue Taxation, which in my opinion is entitled to additional staff members in order to perform its rigorous duties.

For the time being, I leave the Finance Committee, but I shall return to it later in my remarks, when I expect to demonstrate how the Republican establishment cooperates with the Democratic establishment to assure maintenance of the status quo with respect to the number of Senators on certain major committees of the Senate, and show with some glee, because of the dwindling numbers of members of the establishment, that since the election of 1958 it has lost control of a number of major Senate committees.

I believe it is not too much to say that while we may not yet be quite ready for Waterloo in connection with the establishment, we have certainly seen the battle of Moscow lost. Time is on the side of the Presidential party on both sides of the aisle in the Senate. Time is against the aging congressional party, with its dwindling numbers, who are wedded to the status quo.

FOREIGN RELATIONS COMMITTEE

I turn now to a consideration of the situation in the Foreign Relations Committee. Here I must start with a disclaimer. It is well known to my colleagues in the Senate that my overriding ambition for a committee assignment ever since I first came to the Senate 7 years ago has been to be assigned to the Foreign Relations Committee. That ambition has constantly been frustrated, sometimes with the aid of seniority, sometimes in spite of seniority. It therefore may well be felt by my colleagues—and they may well be correct—that in discussing the status of the Foreign Relations Committee I am not entirely objective. All I can say is that I have made an earnest effort to be objective. If I have failed, it has been by reason of human frailty, not because of design.

At the beginning of the session the Foreign Relations Committee consisted of 17 members, with 2 vacancies—in other words, 15 live bodies. The ratio was 11 to 6. Despite the protestations of the chairman of the committee, it was determined to change the ratio to 12 to 5. My own view has been that for reasons of high policy it would be desirabe to change the ratio of the members of the Foreign Relations Committee to 14 to 7, thus making it a 2 to 1 committee, and enlarging it in order to permit additional Members who give bipartisan support to the program of the President overseas in this time of peril to be appointed to the committee from both the Democrat and Republican sides, thereby, hopefully, strengthening a bipartisan approach to foieign affairs, which one would hope might cause partisan politics to stop at the waterfront, as was done in the great days when Senator Vandenberg was the chairman of that committee.

This was not done. One of my amendments to rule XXV which lies at the desk would increase the size of the committee so as to increase the size of the committee to 21. About 1937, when the number of Democratic Senators in this body was even higher than it is today, the Foreign Relations Committee consisted of 23 members. Therefore, there is ample precedent for the suggested change, just as there is for the Finance Committee, as I pointed out yesterday.

I have no complaint whatever about the fact that I was passed over this time in the Foreign Relations Committee, because the able Senator from Florida [Mr. Smathers] had seniority. My complaint is that 2 years ago I was passed over for the Foreign Relations Committee in favor of an equally good friend, who had less seniority, and that 2 years before that I was passed over for the Foreign Relations Committee in favor of two Senators who had no more than equal seniority.

I have tried to be very objective about this situation, and I think I have succeeded. I have no personal quarrel over the action of the steering committee in this regard, which was taken last week, but I have grave concern that on matters such as a test ban treaty, out attitude toward dictatorships in South America and elsewhere, foreign aid and our attitude toward the race issue, by which we are embarrassed in our dealings with Africans and Asians, who believe our policy on the race issue is deplorable. In all these matters I believe it would be helpful if some additional supporters of a bipartisan foreign policy, both Democrats and Republicans, were added to the Foreign Relations Committee.

GOVERNMENT OPERATIONS COMMITTEE

I now turn to the Committee on Government Operations. Here there was no real controversy, because the leadership had determined—and with this I have no quarrel—to make the Government Operations Committee a major committee and to increase its size from 9 to 15 and to maintain a ratio of 2 to 1 in connection with Democratic and Republican members.

There were no applicants for the Committee on Government Operations other than from freshmen Members of the Senate. Generally speaking, they got either this assignment, when they wanted it, or another equally good one. So there was no problem there.

INTERIOR COMMITTEE

Turning to the Committee on Interior and Insular Affairs, we have another situation in which seniority was ignored in favor of two freshmen, thus passing over the Senator from Michigan [Mr. Hart], who will be up for a tough reelection fight in a year and who had seniority, and the Senator from Oregon [Mrs. Neuberger], who also had seniority over the two freshmen Senators who, together with the Senator from Arizona [Mr. Hayden] were assigned to that committee.

Needless to say, when Senator Hayden indicated a desire to join the Committee on Interior and Insular Affairs, the steering committee unanimously granted our beloved President pro tempore this request. But there were still two vacancies left, and they were given to Senator Nelson and Senator McGovern, instead of Senator Hart and Senator Neuberger.

JUDICIARY COMMITTEE

I return to the Committee on the Judiciary, where again, to my way of thinking, a grave injustice was done to one of our finest Senators, Senator Burdick, who will be up for reelection next year. He was most eager to be assigned to the Committee on the Judiciary.

He was passed over by the establishment in favor of two very able freshmen Senators, Senator Kennedy and Senator Bayh. I find little justification for this action on behalf of the establishment. Senator Burdick was really left out in the cold. I do not think a very good case can be made for supporting what the steering committee did in this case.

In all the criticisms I have been making about the actions of the steering committee in overriding and ignoring the seniority rights of what might be called intermediate grade Senators, Senators who came to the Senate in 1958 on the liberal sweep which brought 15 new liberal Democrats and 3 moderate Republicans to the floor of this body, it is my view that those Senators have suffered as a result of the determination of the steering committee not to give to each freshman Senator one good committee, but to give to each freshman Senator two good committees to the prejudice of Senators who are up for reelection next year and who had worked hard in the cause of the President of the United States and had shown by their votes that they were modern Senators, not Senators who are wedded to the status quo.

In each instance, freshmen Senators could have been given another excellent committee, but they were not. They were preferred to Senators like Senator Burdick, who, I believe, had a higher claim on the members of the steering committee.

LABOR AND PUBLIC WELFARE COMMITTEE

I now turn, with mild amusement, to the Committee on Labor and Public Welfare, on which I have the honor to serve, and which I believe to be one of the finest, most important, and most influential committees in the Senate. Senators may recall that yesterday I made the same statement about my other committee, the Committee on Banking and Currency. No Senator wants to be assigned to the Committee on Labor and Public Welfare. Is it not a shame? It is a fine committee. Yet it is not possible to get any Senator to serve on the Committee on Banking and Currency or the Committee on Labor and Public Welfare. Too bad. So the able junior Senator from Massachusetts [Mr. Kennedy] was "shanghaied" and assigned to the Committee on Labor and Public Welfare, even though he did not apply for that committee. However, I am sure he will serve with the same great ability on that committee that his older brother did in the years before he became President of the United States, and when I had the honor to serve with him and bring to the floor of the Senate and have passed much important legislation which we thought then, and I think now, is very much in the public interest.

POST OFFICE AND SERVICE COMMITTEE

I now turn to the Committee on Post Office and Civil Service, from which I resigned after 6 years of interesting service. There again, there was only one applicant, the present occupant of the Chair [Mr. Brewster], and he was assigned to that committee.

It was thought that Senator McGee, of Wyoming, who has a tough campaign for reelection coming up next year, would profit if he were able to have the close association with the members of the Civil Service and particularly of the Post Office Department which that committee would give him. He was placed on that committee; and there was, of course, no real controversy.

PUBLIC WORKS COMMITTEE

The next committee is the Committee on Public Works. There again we have an interesting situation. The membership of that committee is 17, and the ratio had been 11 Democrats and 6 Republicans. The ratio was changed to 12 to 5. This resulted in five vacancies on that committee—a very large number of vacancies.

Senator Jordan of North Carolina was not an applicant for assignment to that committee; but he had seniority, and he was assigned to the committee for the very good reason that there were at that time no Senators from the South who were members of that important committee. In this instance, seniority was honored, and Senator Jordan was placed on that committee.

Then, in quick succession, Senator Brewster, Senator Inouye, Senator Bayh, and Senator Nelson were placed on that committee, jumping over Senator McIntyre, of New Hampshire, who had seniority by about 2 months.

Let it not be thought that the question of seniority by a day or two or a month or two has not hitherto been important. It has. I have seen many instances since I came to the Senate in which Senators who had seniority of not more than 3 or 4 days over their colleagues were automatically accorded that seniority right when it came to the question not only of their assignment to a committee, but also of their priority on that committee in terms of seniority once they got there.

But the Senator from New Hampshire [Mr. McIntyre] was ignored, and other fine and able junior Senators, including the present occupant of the chair, the junior Senator from Maryland [Mr. Brewster], were placed on that committee. I am sure that those Senators will render fine service. I am confident that the four freshmen are Kennedy men, are liberals, and will support the administration. My only complaint was, and is, that I thought it was a little rough on Senator McIntyre, who is in the same category and desired to be assigned to the Committee on Public Works.

RULES AND ADMINISTRATION COMMITTEE

The final committee is the Committee on Rules and Administration. In this instance, there is a rather amusing little interlude. That committee had been changed from a major committee to a minor committee by prior action of the steering committee at the time we came to a vote. Senators will recall that I am committed not to reveal the vote on the filling of committee vacancies, and I shall not do so. But the order of seniority of applicants for that committee was: Senator Thurmond, of South Carolina, whose seniority dates from November 7, 1956; I, whose seniority dates from 2 months later, January 3, 1957; Senator Byrd of West Virginia, whose seniority dates from January 7, 1959; and Senator Neuberger, of Oregon, whose seniority dates from November 9, 1960.

When the secret ballots were counted, it was discovered that the Senator from West Virginia [Mr. Byrd] had won selection to the committee. The second choice was so divided that no Senator had a majority; but the two highest on the list were the Senator from Oregon [Mrs. Neuberger] and I. The Senator from South Carolina [Mr. Thurmond], who had seniority over all of us, was, therefore, dropped from further consideration; and the balloting then took place between the Senator from Oregon [Mrs. Neuberger] and myself. I am selfishly pleased that in that very close race, I received the nod; and I thank some of my friends from the establishment for their graciousness in helping me in that way to achieve membership on the committee, because at the time when the vote was taken, I had been engaged in about a 2-hour battle to achieve results in other instances—athough in each case I had failed. So I am grateful, indeed, that I have been selected for appointment to the Committee on Rules and Administration. Having received that choice, I shall do my very best as a member of the Committee on Rules and Administration to change—drastically—the Senate rules, in order to update the procedures of the Senate and its ability to conduct its business expeditiously.

This completes my initial review of the actions of the steering committee. I recapitulate by saying that in making its choices, the steering committee ignored seniority nine times, in order to give freshman Senators assignments to two major committees— not merely one—although it could have given them assignments to two major committees without in any instance overriding the requests of intermediate Senators of substantially greater seniority, and jumping nonfreshman Senators over other nonfreshman Senators who had seniority, notably in the cases of the Senator from Alaska [Mr. Bartlett], who was assigned to the Appropriations Committee, and myself, who was assigned—as the second choice—to the Committee on Rules and Administration, and also in the case of the assignment of the Senator from West Virginia [Mr. Byrd] to the Committee on Rules and Administration. I make clear that I am not complaining about my own selection for membership on the Committee on Rules and Administration.

Yesterday the Senator from Wisconsin [Mr. Proxmire]—whom I see in the Chamber—made an eloquent plea for the rule of seniority in the selection of Members to be assigned to committees, with the sole exception of cases in which it was necessary to ignore seniority in order to assign freshman Senators to one major committee. At that time I undertook to differ with him. I should like to state now the reasons why I took that position.

It seems to me that in the area of the selection of committee members we should have representative government within the organization of both the Republican Party and the Democratic Party. We should choose for appointment to the committees, Members in whom we have confidence—confidence that they will do the right thing, as they see it, while they serve on the steering committee. I do not question that the present members of the steering committee thought they were doing the right thing, although I disagree with them. Nevertheless, I do not impugn in any way their motives. Furthermore, the steering committee should be composed of Senators who fairly represent the ideology and the geography of the members of the Democratic conference; and after having so chosen the members on an equitable basis, we should be prepared to permit them to make the initial choice of the Members to fill committee vacancies.

I would go along with the Senator from Oregon [Mr. Morse] —and I did so in the ballot within the Democratic conference— in taking the position that in each instance the Democratic conference should have the right to change the recommendations of the steering committee before the lists are submitted to the Senate. That would be only sound democratic procedure, just as it conforms with the practice on the floor of the Senate, where the Senate itself checks, amends, rejects, or approves the recommendations of all the committees which deal with legislation. But, even if we could not obtain this review by the Democratic conference of the recommendations of the steering committee, I would be prepared to leave the members of the steering committee rather free as to their choices, subject to the general criteria. It seems to me that those criteria, which would usually—although not always—prevail, would be that in making their selections, the members of the committee, acting—I am sure—in good faith, would take into account seniority, geography, ideology, competence, and experience; and they should try to get—within the broad outlines of those general criteria—the very best Members available within the whole body of the Democratic side of the Senate, to serve on the particular committees in which vacancies occur.

I would not want any more rigorous ground rule than that. Of course, in order to make it effective, it would be necessary to have a representative steering committee. Although, as I have been pointing out, the present steering committee is not representative in terms of either ideology or geography, I would say to the Senator from Wisconsin [Mr. Proxmire] that all we need, in order to get the kind of steering committee which he and I would like to have, is the support of the leadership. Until we came to the Democratic conference the other day, I had hoped we would have the support of the leadership in the attempt to increase the size of the steering committee to either 19 or 17; and 2 years ago I was given to understand—although no commitment was made—that there would be resignations from the steering committee, from among the members from the Deep South, in order to make it possible to comply with the requirement—laid down in both 1961 and 1963—by the Democratic conference that the membership of the steering committee should represent both the geography and the ideology of the members of the conference. I say to the Senator from Wisconsin that I have not despaired of getting the leadership to change its mind in that regard.

I am telling no tales out of school when I say that within the leadership itself there is dissention on this point. I would hope that the majority leader and the whip would in due course conclude that the commitment made to the Democratic conference in 1961 and 1963 should be kept.

I point out to my friend from Wisconsin that we were not too far away from winning anyway, even with the opposition of the leadership. We got 21 votes out of 60, for a steering committee of 19. We got 23 votes out of 60 for a steering committee of 17. A shift of only 10 votes would have changed the result. If the leadership were to shift, there is not a shadow of doubt in my mind that the majority would shift, too.

I point out that there were only 60 votes, because 7 Democratic Senators were unable to attend the conference.

MR. PROXMIRE   Mr. President, will the Senator yield?

MR. CLARK   I yield to my friend from Wisconsin.

MR. PROXMIRE   With much of what the Senator has said today I wholeheartedly agree. Of course, the body of his speech I find agreeable. Also I concur with his statement that he thinks the steering committee should be guided by criteria. That is very important. Perhaps those criteria exist implicitly. I do not know of any explicit statement that seniority, geography, ideology, and competence should be considered. If there is such a generalized notion, I do not believe it is widely understood.

MR. CLARK   Clearly or not, consider what happened.

MR. PROXMIRE Very well; consider what happened. Let me discuss with the Senator from Pennsylvania what course ought to be followed. The Senator has said he thinks we were close to victory because we got 21 votes in the caucus of 60 Senators.

MR. CLARK Twenty-three.

MR. PROXMIRE That was for 19 members of the steering committee; and 23 votes for 17 members of the steering committee. I submit that if there were 19 members on the steering committee, it would not have made any difference on any vote the Senator has discussed today.

Without having had revealed to me the precise vote, I understand that it was pretty substantial. It was not even close. I would not say there was a "snow job," but there was an overwhelming decision made by those members of the steering committee. Assuming that the new members of the steering committee would all tend to agree with the Senator from Pennsylvania or the Senator from Wisconsin, I still think it is very doubtful that it would have made any real difference in the voting of the steering committee.

MR. CLARK Mr. President, if the Senator will permit me to interrupt, I respectfully disagree with my friend from Wisconsin. I am interested that my friend should have referred to that snow which falls with such plentitude on the marvelous forests and farmlands of his home State. Off the floor of the Senate I have said—and I say now in a mildly lighter vein, impugning neither the motives nor the action of any Senator—that what happened was the greatest "snow job" since the blizzard of 1888. I marvel at the efficiency with which that snow fell.

To get back to the other point, I am confident that if the composition of the steering committee had been readjusted so as to make it conform to the geography and ideology of the Senate, and if it had consisted of 19 members, there is no doubt that the results for which the Senator and I jointly contend would have been achieved. If the number had been 17, the issue would have been more doubtful. But, after all, there was only a hard core of seven votes that might not have been shifted if the composition of the committee had been otherwise. At the very most there were nine. With a committee of 19, I think we would have won 10 to 9 if the issue had been forced in each case.

MR. PROXMIRE At any rate, whether or not the Senator would have prevailed if he got the kind of composition of the steering committee for which he asked is certainly subject to question, because we do not know who would have been nominated by the leadership and who would have been approved by the caucus. We do not know exactly what views they would have taken on this particular vote.

The point that the Senator from Wisconsin wishes to make is—

MR. CLARK Mr. President, if the Senator will permit me to interrupt briefly before he continues, since I am afraid I shall lose the floor, I should like to point out that I believe time is on our side.

I hope the Senator from Wisconsin will be returned to this body by an overwhelming majority next year. I have 6 more years myself. I am hopeful that our friends in the class of 1958, in the class of 1960, and in the class of 1962 will be here for many more years. I do not believe the attrition in that group will be very high. Let us be patient.

MR. PROXMIRE Mr. President, will the Senator yield?

MR. CLARK I yield.

MR. PROXMIRE I have enough appreciation of the two-party system and of the ebb and flow of party fortunes to anticipate that it will be unlikely in the future that we shall continue to have 67 Democrats in the Senate, or a 2-to-1 relationship with the Republicans. I suspect that a time will come when there may be a majority of Republicans. When that time comes, I suppose that most of us from the North will no longer be here. Our southern brethren are likely to be here, if they live that long. If not, they will be succeeded by Senators who will have an equally long term of service in the Senate.

MR. CLARK I point out that when those Senators are succeeded by other southern Senators, the new southern Senators will not have seniority.

MR. PROXMIRE Yes; but if we take the long sweep of American history—certainly for the past 100 years—there is no question that in the Democratic Party southern Senators have had seniority. Furthermore, there have been many periods in which southern Senators have had close to a majority of Democratic Senators.

We should anticipate that southern Senators will have seniority, and in certain periods will have close to a majority of all Democratic Senators, as they had even as recently as 1947 and 1948.

MR. CLARK   The Senator refers to all Democratic Senators.

MR. PROXMIRE   All Democratic Senators. So they will be able to control the Democratic conference absolutely, even without any allies.

MR. CLARK   If I may interrupt the Senator, I should like to point out that as a result of the activities of northern and western Democrats, joined by a perceptible handful of Republicans, we are gradually enfranchising the Negro in the South.

MR. PROXMIRE   Mr. President, will the Senator yield?

MR. CLARK   I yield.

MR. PROXMIRE   The day may come when we shall have a two-party system in South Carolina and Mississippi. But I did not want to base our hopes in achieving appointments to committees on a possible two-party system in those States and in other Southern States.

MR. CLARK   The Senator misunderstands me. I am not so much thinking about a two-party system, although personally I would like to see it. I am thinking of a drastic revision in the thinking of Senators from the South, once the Negro is really enfranchised and comes to be—as he is frequently in my Commonwealth of Pennsylvania today—the deciding factor in a close election.

MR. PROXMIRE   I agree that such a development is likely to take place sooner that the development of a two-party system in the South. It seems to me on the basis of the experience we have had that we can anticipate a situation in which those who were inclined to disagree with the viewpoint of the Senator from Pennsylvania and the Senator from Wisconsin on civil rights will have disproportionate power in the Democratic Party, considering their numbers. They will have disproportionate representation on the steering committee.

MR. CLARK   They do today.

MR. PROXMIRE   There will be disproportionate influence on

the steering committee. Whether it consists of 17 members or 19, they will continue to have exceptional influence, not only because of their numbers, but because of their ability and experience. Recognizing that we are likely to have a steering committee which will have disproportionate representation of Southern Senators for the forseeable future, it seems to me it is the better part of wisdom on our part to insist upon the most objective criteria for appointments to committees that we can win. We cannot rely on a favorable steering committee. We must therefore rely on criteria that will require fairness and objective appointment by the steering committee.

I submit that we should be able to win, without any question, approval of an objective criteria like seniority from members of the steering committee. If they will not accept it, it seems to me they are wrong and we can take the issue to our constituency, to the country, or anywhere we may wish to take it and convince the people that we are right and the other Members are wrong. Appointments to the various committees of the Senate should be made on the same basis on which appointments of chairmen of committees and subcommittees are made, except that appointments of new Senators to a major committee shall be an exception; and if other exceptions are made there should be a clear written explanation of the reason. That written explanation might be on the basis of geography, or perhaps on the basis of an ideological imbalance on the committee. It might be on the basis of exceptional competence, although I do not think one would find much justification on that basis, no matter how it was stated, because everybody feels that all Senators are competent, and nobody is going to make a public argument that any Senator is incompetent or less competent than someone else.

I submit that if we try to stick as close as we can to seniority then we can avoid the kind of thing which happened with respect to the Appropriations Committee this year, when a fine Senator, with less seniority, but who voted with the southerners in the crucial vote over the filibuster—was given the appointment to this prize, prime committee over two other Senators with more seniority; one who voted against the southerners consistently on the filibuster, from the North, and one who showed exceptional courage and independence and frequently disagrees with his southern brethren. I refer to the Senator from Texas [Mr. Yarborough].

MR. CLARK Will the Senator permit me to interrupt?

MR. PROXMIRE The point the Senator wishes to stress is that when we have a committee stacked against us making the appointments—stacked against us on the basis of elections from the South, or ideological attitudes, or whatever one wishes to call it —we need the clearest and simplest criterion we can get, applied with scrupulous fairness and justice, and applied in such a way that we can always take our case to other Senators, or take our case to members of the steering committee themselves, to say, "I have seniority over my contender for this position, and should be given the appointment." If we have that protection we will be considered fairly. If we do not have it, it seems to me that the Senator from Pennsylvania has made a devastating case that we can expect to lose out.

MR. CLARK If the Senator's premise is correct, his conclusion is entirely sound. I challenge the premise, for the reasons I outlined a few minutes ago.

Nevertheless, the Senator's suggested criterion, if adopted, would certainly be far better than the situation under which we now operate. Until such time as we can successfully readjust the membership of the steering committee to meet ideology and geography, as, in effect, the conference directed, I would support the Senator.

MR. PROXMIRE I thank the Senator very much. With the exception which has been mentioned—of the newly elected Senators appointed to committees regardless of seniority—the steering committee now generally follows the policy of seniority. It does make exceptions, however. When it makes exceptions, I think we ought to insist on justification. After all, it is our steering committee. We appoint the members. Why should we let them get away with it? Why should we not insist that they make an explanation, either to the Senate or to the caucus, as to why they wish to appoint A over B, when B has seniority over A? They ought to have a reason for it, other than the fact that they like B better.

MR. CLARK   Let me point out to my friend from Wisconsin that he will have an opportunity on the floor of the Senate to do exactly that next Monday. Perhaps he was not in the Chamber when that was arranged.

MR. PROXMIRE   I understand that, but I say to the Senator from Pennsylvania that these things are always extremely awkward. When any Senator stands—particularly one who feels he has not gotten his just due—and asks, "Why was I not given this assignment instead of another Senator?" it is extremely embarassing. All those who are involved are embarassed. Senators do not like to do that.

If this criterion were written into the rules, and if it were required that the steering committee, if it made this kind of exception, would have to give its reasons, in most cases we would have an objective and fair criterion of seniority applied. That would be true in most instances, except when the discrimination was based on some good, solid, sound justifiable reason like a gross geographical or ideological imbalance of the kind we now have on the Interior and Insular Affairs Committee.

MR. CLARK   I am sure my friend from Wisconsin does not think I was without embarrassment when I began to make this detailed speech.

MR. PROXMIRE   The Senator is correct, but I am sure the Senator from Pennsylvania has one great advantage. It is very clear that the Senator is not seeking in any way to serve his own interests in making the speech. However, if the Senator from Wisconsin or the Senator from Texas should protest the appointment of the Senator from Alaska to the Committee on Appropriations over their senior claims, it would be taken, I think, by many people in the Senate and outside the Senate as coming with bad grace. It is something which is not done. For that reason, we would be in a different position from that occupied by the Senator from Pennsylvania, who has shown extraordinary courage and conviction in making the fine fight he has made.

MR. CLARK   Let me say to my friend from Wisconsin that I am sure there will be some—perhaps many—who will say that the reason I am making this speech is that I was disappointed over not being appointed to the Committee on Foreign Relations.

I have undertaken to lay that ghost, whether successfully or not I do not know.

The Senator from Wisconsin could rise on the floor on Monday to challenge the ignoring of seniority in each of the nine cases in which he was not personally involved. How, then, could anyone say he was trying to feather his own nest?

MR. PROXMIRE I say to the Senator from Pennsylvania that I do not like to suggest a statistic which weakens our case, but in view of that challenge I do not know how to avoid it. The fact is that there were only two cases in which seniority was ignored except in the cases of junior Senators given more than one committee; those two exceptions were first, the Appropriations Committee assignment; and secondly the assignment to the Committee on Rules and Administration, to which the Senator from Pennsylvania was appointed over the Senator from South Carolina.

These assignments violated seniority. There has been no jurisdiction, no explanation for it. There should be. If a junior member of a committee were made chairman, the Senate and the senior Members passed over would deserve an explanation. They would get it. These two exceptions deserve explanation too. Why don't we get one?

MR. CLARK I do not know.

MR. PROXMIRE At any rate, I am not inclined to make a fight either with respect to the Appropriations Committee or the Committee on Rules and Administration under the present circumstances; and the other decisions were made in favor of the freshmen Senators.

MR. CLARK Perhaps we could more profitably continue our discussion some other time.

MR. PROXMIRE I think so.

MR. CLARK Mr. President, I turn briefly to the question of packing and stacking and shuffling.

There have been those who have suggested that liberal Senators wanted to pack committees. I suppose the analogy was to the Roosevelt attempt to pack the Supreme Court.

An effort has been made to make the Senator from Pennsylvania appear, indeed, mildly unethical, because he wants to change the size of these committees to put supporters of the

President of the United States, to put able and experienced Democratic Senators who sought these assignments, on particular committees.

I think I have cited enough precedents in the history of the Senate, when the size of committees has been changed, to meet the contingencies of the day. In no instance have I asked that any committee be increased in size larger than it had been in the past, except the Appropriations Committee, with respect to which a special condition existed reflecting the "bumping."

Moreover, we are playing now, not with a packed deck, but with a stacked deck. The deck is stacked against the President of the United States, and I want to shuffle that deck so that in the end the President of the United States will have his fair share of trumps and we can play the game with an honest deck of cards.

I immediately again want to say that I am not accusing anybody of dishonesty. I am not accusing anybody of improper motives. I am not accusing anyone of doing anything other than desiring to retain the status quo. But the status quo is a stacked deck, and all I am trying to do is unstack it, and I do not think the comment that this involves packing the committee has much justification.

REPUBLICAN MEMBERS OF THE ESTABLISHMENT

Mr. President, having said my fair share—perhaps more than my fair share—about the Democratic side of the Senate establishment, I should like to say a few words about their allies, the Republican Members of the Senate establishment. This is a small and dwindling group of supporters of the status quo.

I can remember, when I first came to the Senate, there were 47 Republicans here. That number, I am happy to say, has now been reduced to 33, and among those 33 is a small but active and able group of liberal Republican Senators. But the dwindling group of establishment Republicans is still essential to the establishment of the Senate and those devoted to the status quo.

It is only with the aid of the able and beloved minority leader, the champion of the Republican establishment, that our friends in the Democratic establishment have been able to retain that control of key committees which is essential to the slowing down, if not the defeat, of major progressive proposals of the President of the United States.

I shall not name names, but I shall ask my colleagues to look carefully at the membership of the Appropriations Committee, and I make the suggestion that the bipartisan, conservative, status quo establishment presently controls the Appropriations Committee by a very narrow margin; and that if it had been increased in number to 29 from 27, and the Senator from New York had been left on it from the Republican side, and a liberal Democrat with seniority who had been applying for the job had been placed on it, the establishment might have lost control of the Appropriations Committee, so razor thin is their control at the moment.

Let us look at the Committee on Armed Services. There the establishment is in command, with the help of the Republicans.

MR. PROXMIRE   Mr. President, will the Senator yield on the point of the Appropriations Committee?

MR. CLARK   I am happy to yield.

MR. PROXMIRE   One shocking imbalance on the Appropriations Committee is that eight of the subcommittees of the Appropriations Committee have as chairmen southerners—two-thirds, 2 to 1.

MR. CLARK   The Senator is correct.

MR. PROXMIRE   Here I think is a striking example of the domination of the policies of the Congress of the United States, or at least the U.S. Senate, by one area of the country. I think this is an element of appropriation control and of power that has been overlooked.

None of us is challenging the right of senior southerners to whatever position they are entitled to; but how very moderate and mild is the position taken by the Senator from Pennsylvania. All he is asking is that in committee assignments some consideration be given—equal and fair consideration—to Senators who are not from the South. We recognize the enormous power the southerners have. We are not trying to undermine it or even challenge it; we are simply asking for fair consideration under the rules which southerners champion and which suit their purposes very well.

MR. CLARK   I thank the Senator from Wisconsin.

I now turn to the vital assistance of the Republican members of the establishment in maintaining control of the Armed Services Committee, a committee very important indeed to our national security.

I think, in fairness, it might be pointed out that when the establishment gets into military affairs, they do not hold back. I want to be careful in the choice of my words, so as not to give affront. But certainly the establishment in its control of the Armed Services Committee is not notorious in its support of the present or past administration's efforts to obtain test ban and disarmament agreements with the Soviets. I am sure this position is sincere, but I point out that that committee, as anyone who wishes to run his eye down its membership will inevitably conclude, is controlled by a bipartisan coalition of the establishment which, I do not believe, when the chips are down, will give support to certain efforts by the President to ameliorate the cold war situation, or to curtail that military and industrial complex which President Eisenhower referred to. I do not think we are going to get much support from that committee on those matters, which I believe to be in the public interest.

The next committee which the Republicans are responsible for aiding the conservative Democrats in completely controlling is the Finance Committee. I see an able member of that committee, the Senator from Illinois [Mr. Douglas], on the floor. I am certain he will agree with me that the most fairminded and objective observer, as he runs his eye down the membership of the Finance Committee, will inevitably conclude that the bipartisan establishment has a majority of that committee firmly in its grasp, to the detriment of the program of the President of the United States.

MR. DOUGLAS   Mr. President, will the Senator yield?

MR. CLARK.   I am happy to yield to the Senator from Illinois.

MR. DOUGLAS   Since an implicit question has been asked of me, I would say in years past that has been the case. We hope it will not be the case in the future. Certainly it is a true statement of what has happened in the past.

MR. CLARK   I should like to point out that even in the Finance

Committee there is a slow attrition working against the bipartisan establishment. Its control of the Finance Committee was far greater some years ago—in fact, when I first came to the Senate—than it is today. If we can increase the size of the Finance Committee, as I have suggested, we can probably wrest control of that committee from the establishment, and thus add it to the large number of other committees over which the establishment has lost control.

The next committee of which the establishment has control is the Foreign Relations Committee. There I must tread lightly, first, because of my own personal interest in the matter, and second, because the field of foreign relations is very complicated and complex, involving shifts, depending upon the particular issue, in the attitude and position of members of that committee.

I will make the statement that on the whole, and all things considered, as a result of the two new appointments which are being made to that committee, the program of the President in foreign affairs is in jeopardy so far as that program is under the control of the Foreign Relations Committee.

The next committee is the Committee on Rules and Administration. I see my friend the Senator from Rhode Island [Mr. Pell] on the floor. He is an able member of the Committee on Rules and Administration. I point out that one sardonic thing about what happened is that the control of the establishment over the Rules Committee has now shrunk to a 5 to 4 majority.

I believe the Senator from Rhode Island and I have some hope that with the aid of our fine new Republican colleagues, the Senator from Kentucky [Mr. Cooper] and the Senator from Pennsylvania [Mr. Scott], we might just be able to persuade a majority of the committee to bring to the floor of the Senate some badly needed changes in our rules and procedures, for which the Senator from Rhode Island and I have been contending.

To sum up this portion of my talk, I emphasize the fact that this control of the establishment over the Senate requires the support of a dwindling group of Republican conservatives headed by the able and distinguished minority leader, and that as a result of what has happened since the election of 1958, when

18 forward-looking, modern Senators joined this body, and the election of 1960, when the Senator from Rhode Island and several other Senators joined this body, and now because of the election of 1962, when a substantial group of splendid forward-looking liberal Senators joined the Senate, the attrition on the establishment has been very substantial indeed.

Let me point out that since 1958 the establishment has lost control of the Banking and Currency Committee, the Commerce Committee, the Committee on Government Operations, the Interior Committee, and, as of Monday believe it or not, the Judiciary Committee. They never had control of the Committee on Labor and Public Welfare. They have lost control of the Public Works Committee.

Therefore time is on our side. Unless catastrophe overtakes the liberals of both parties in the election of 1964, I predict that we are within striking distance of obtaining control of the committee system of the Senate for the liberal and forward-looking elements on both sides of the aisle.

Yesterday the majority leader, as reported at page 2424 of the *Congressional Record,* asked me to comment on whether the actions of the steering committee had revealed a constant pattern of bias in favor of junior Senators who had voted against cloture and to overlook the claim of Senators, frequently of greater seniority, who had voted for cloture. At that time I refused to make a statement one way or the other because I wanted to assemble the facts.

To my mind it would serve no useful purpose for me to make any charge or any statement one way or the other. However I have had prepared a table which shows the names of Senators on the Democratic side who sought committee assignments, what their first, second, and third choices were, and the position they took either for or against a change in rule XXII, and therefore, almost automatically, the position they took on cloture.

I will state only facts. I will not draw any conclusions. First I ask unanimous consent that a copy of the compilation prepared for me by my staff may be printed in the *Record* at this point.

There being no objection, the table was ordered to be printed in the *Record,* as follows:

STAFF MEMORANDUM TO SENATOR CLARK

Twenty-two nonfreshman Democratic Senators submitted eligible[1] bids for new committee assignments as shown below. The committees received, if any, and the position of each Senator on the rule XXII question, are indicated also.

Name	Committee assignments received	Choice	Position on rule XXII	
			For change	Against change
Bartlett	Appropriations	1st	.....	X
Burdick	None	....	X	
Byrd (W. Virginia).	Rules	No. 1 eligible.	.....	X
Cannon	Commerce (applied for Commerce and Finance)..	....	.....	X
Clark	Rules	No. 2 ...	X	
Engle	None	....	X	
Hart	Commerce	No. 3 ...	X	
Hayden	Interior	No. 1 ...	.....	X
Jordan	Public Works	No. 1 ...	.....	X
Lausche	None	....	X	
Long (Missouri) ...	....do	....	X	
McGee	Post Office and Civil Service	No. 1 ...	.....	X
Moss	None	....	X	
Mansfield	Appropriations	No. 1 ...	X	
Muskie	None	....	X	
Neuberger	....do	....	X	
Pell	Government Operations	No. 2 ...	X	
Proxmire	None	....	X	
Smathers	Foreign Relations	No. 1 ...	.....	X
Thurmond ...	None	....	.....	X
Yarborough ..	....do	....	X	
Young (Ohio)	Armed Services	No. 2 ...	X	

[1] Ineligible bids for the Space Committee were submitted by Senators Byrd of West Virginia, Monroney, and Sparkman.

CONCLUSIONS

1. Eight nonfreshmen Senators (Bartlett, Byrd, Cannon, Hayden, Jordan, McGee, Smathers, Thurmond) who opposed rules change submitted eligible bids for new committee assignments. Seven of them (88 percent) got new assignments. Six (75 percent) got the assignments which represented their first choice (only Thurmond was disappointed).

2. Fourteen nonfreshmen Senators who favored rules change applied for new committee assignments. Five (36 percent) got new assignments (Mansfield, Hart, Pell, Young, and Clark); only one Senator (7 percent) of the group—Senator Mansfield—got the committee which was his first choice.

MR. CLARK   Mr. President, one who analyzes this statement for the purpose of determining the ultimate facts will see that eight nonfreshman Senators who opposed a rules change submitted eligible bids for new committee assignments. Seven of the eight got new assignments. Six of the eight got new assignments which represented their first choice. Fourteen nonfreshman Senators who favored a rules change applied for new assignments. These were men who had voted for cloture. Five of the fourteen got new assignments. Only one got the committee of his first choice, and that was the majority leader.

MR. PROXMIRE   Mr. President, will the Senator yield? This is a startling analysis.

MR. CLARK   I will yield in a moment. These facts speak for themselves, and I will not draw any conclusions therefrom. I want to be very careful not to make any charges which will either inflame good friends of mine or result in my being charged with misrepresenting the facts. I now yield to the Senator from Wisconsin.

MR. PROXMIRE   The Senator says that eight nonfreshman Senators who opposed a rules change and supported the South submitted eligible bids for new committee assignments, and that seven of those eight got new assignments, and that six out of the eight, or three-fourths, got their first choice.

MR. CLARK   The Senator is correct. This appears in the table that I have placed in the *Record*. The only nonfreshman Senator in this category who was disappointed was the Senator from South Carolina [Mr. Thurmond].

MR. PROXMIRE   Then the Senator says that 14 nonfreshmen

Senators who favored a rules change applied for new committee assignments, and that in sharp contrast, whereas among those who voted with the South on rules change 88 percent, or 7 out of 8 had gotten an assignment they sought, of those who voted against the South only 5 or nearly 36 percent, or 1 out of 3, got any new assignment.

MR. CLARK   I might comment on that. The five were Senator Mansfield, who applied for Appropriations, and of course the majority leader was unanimously given this choice, which he deserved in terms of seniority; Senator Hart, of Michigan, who, as I pointed out earlier, was saved by the bell from getting no new committee assignment at all; Senator Pell, who was shanghaied and given a committee he did not want to serve on, although I am sure he will render very valuable service there; Senator Young of Ohio, who got his second choice; and I, who squeaked onto the Rules Committee by the skin of my teeth.

MR. PROXMIRE   Only one of those Senators, or 1 out of 14, got the committee which was his first choice, and that was the majority leader. Is that correct?

MR. CLARK   The Senator is correct.

MR. PROXMIRE   The majority leader.

MR. CLARK   Yes.

MR. PROXMIRE   In other words, of all the Senators applying for a committee assignment in the entire Senate who opposed the South, only the majority leader out of the 14 got his first choice. In other words, all the others were turned down, whereas of the Senators who had voted with the South, six out of eight got their first choice. Is that correct?

MR. CLARK   That's correct. I have to add a footnote, which is in the analysis I placed in the *Record,* that this compilation excludes the bids of Senators who were ineligible for the committee seats they sought because they already had so many that they could not be assigned to another one. Those Senators were: Byrd of West Virginia, Monroney, and Sparkman.

MR. PROXMIRE   Then there was another elimination, which reinforces the objectivity of this analysis, and that is that the freshman Senators were eliminated from consideration in this particular analysis.

It was my feeling that many freshman Senators, regardless of seniority, should have been given their choice committees. The Senator from Pennsylvania properly left that out of his considerations. All the Senator from Pennsylvania is considering is why those Senators, not freshmen, failed to receive choice committee assignments. It seems to me the facts of the Senator from Pennsylvania are simply devastating in support—the Senator from Pennsylvania is not saying this: I am—of the position which I understood the Senator from Illinois [Mr. Douglas] to take the other day, when he said that it may well be—I do not want to put words in his mouth, either—that there was some consideration of the vote on rule XXII when the committee assignments were made. I do not know how anybody can read these figures without feeling that perhaps this is true.

MR. CLARK   I make no charge; I have just stated the facts.

With respect to the freshman Senators, I point out that this resolution was not dependent in any way on giving them one first-class committee assignment. In my opinion, it could have been worked out so that they could have received two first-class committee assignments and still not have disappointed so many nonfreshman Senators in their ambitions.

Mr. President, I have several other matters to discuss; but because of the lateness of the hour, I shall terminate my discussion at this point and resume it tomorrow.

I thank the Senator from Illinois and the Senator from Wisconsin for their helpful intervention.

I yield the floor.

February 21, 1963

MR. CLARK   Mr. President, I turn to the concluding portion of my remarks on the Senate establishment.

It will be recalled that yesterday I placed in the *Record*—at page 2530—a table outlining the names of certain Senators who had requested various committee assignments as their first, second, or third choice, and compared the committee assignments they actually received—if any—with their position for or against a change in rule XXII, to enable the Senate to terminate unlimited debate by a smaller number of votes than those presently required under that rule. The factual conclusion which this table demonstrates is that eight nonfreshmen Senators—Senators Bartlett, Byrd of West Virginia, Cannon, Hayden, Jordan of North Carolina, McGee, Smathers, and Thurmond—who opposed a change in rule XXII, submitted eligible bids for new committee assignments, and seven of those eight received the new committee assignments they had requested. Six received committee assignments which represented their first choice. Only the Senator from South Carolina [Mr. Thurmond] was disappointed.

On the other hand, 14 nonfreshman Senators who favored a change in rule XXII, and therefore favored cloture, applied for new committee assignments. Only five of them received them. Those Senators were Senators Mansfield, Hart, Pell, Young of Ohio, and myself. The Senator from Montana [Mr. Mansfield], the majority leader, received his first choice. The Senator from Michigan [Mr. Hart] received his third choice. The Senator from Rhode Island [Mr. Pell] received a committee assignment which he did not request and did not want. The Senator from Ohio [Mr. Young] received his second choice. I received my second choice.

I drew no conclusion from that statement. However, I think it raises some interesting speculations.

I should like now to continue my theme that the South is overrepresented in the committee structure of the Senate in terms of geography and also in terms of the ideological convictions of Members on the Democratic side of the Senate. The overrepresentation has resulted from the strict carrying out of that rule of seniority which the steering committee so frequently violated—on nine committees to be exact—in the course of making committee assignments for the present session of Congress.

I ask unanimous consent that a brief statement showing the overrepresentation may be printed in the *Record* at this point as a part of my remarks.

There being no objection, the statement was ordered to be printed in the *Record,* as follows:

SOUTHERN CONTROL OF KEY SENATE COMMITTEES

There are 23 Democratic Senators from the South, including the 11 States of the Confederacy and Oklahoma and Arkansas. The southern Senators make up 34 percent of the 67-man Democratic block in the Senate at present. The 23 Senators from the South have far more than 34 percent of the seats on the 4 most important standing committees of the Senate, however, and more than their share of the seats of the Democratic leadership committees.

Committee	Southern seats	Entitled	Overrepresentation
Appropriations	9 (50 percent) out of 18....	6	3
Armed Services	5 (42 percent) out of 12....	4	1
Finance	6 (55 percent) out of 11....	4	2
Foreign Relations	5 (42 percent) out of 12....	4	1
Policy	3 (33 percent) out of 9.....	3	0
Steering	7 (47 percent) out of 15....	5	2

MR. CLARK   It will be noted that 50 percent of the members of the Democratic representation on the Appropriations Committee are southern Senators; 42 percent are on the Committee on Armed Services; 55 percent are on the Committee on Finance; 42 percent are on the Committee on Foreign Relations; 47 percent are on the steering committee.

I make the comment, not in criticism of any southern Senator, for surely they are entitled to press their own claims for membership on important committees. I make the comment only to show the extent to which the Senate establishment, led by Senators from the South, but very ably abetted by northern Senators of the Republican Party, led by the intrepid minority leader, has a stranglehold on the four most important legislative committees —Appropriations, Armed Services, Finance, and Foreign Relations—and on the very important Democratic steering committee. It is my contention that if we are to advance the program of the President and do justice to the fair claims of Senators from other sections of the country or of a different ideology, the stranglehold of the bipartisan Senate establishment must eventually be broken; and I believe it will eventually be.

I turn now to the proposed change in rule XXV, which is set forth in Senate Resolution 90, cosponsored by the majority and the minority leaders. That proposed rule would change the existing rule in a number of particulars. It would make the Committee on Government Operations a major committee and increase its size from 9 to 15. To that I have no objection. It would make the Committee on Aeronautical and Space Sciences a major committee. That should have been done at the time that committee was established. Failure to do so has entrenched Members of the establishment in an additional area, since aeronautical and space sciences have become a pertinent matter for a legislative committee. So, of course, I have no objection whatever to that change.

The change would also make the Committee on Rules and Administration a minor committee instead of a major committee. I have no quarrel with that. It has enabled me to become a member of the Committee on Rules and Administration for which I otherwise would not have been eligible.

GRANDFATHER CLAUSE IN SENATE RESOLUTION 90

But I should like to point out what the changes do in terms of creating what we might call a preferred list of Senators. I should like to call attention to the so-called grandfather clause, which has been interjected into the rule under the joint leadership of the majority and minority leaders.

Some of us are old enough to remember the derivation of the "grandfather" clause. It was utilized by my southern ancestors from Louisiana shortly after the Civil War. My great grandfather, Daniel Dudley Avery, and my grandfather, Dudley Avery, were both supporters of the Confederacy. They and their Reconstruction day companions utilized the grandfather clause to prevent the Negro from voting. I suggest that the grandfather clause is being utilized today in the Senate for a not entirely dissimilar purpose. But it is a rather obscure purpose and requires some clarification. The grandfather clause as it appears in Senate Resolution 90 provides that—

> *Provided, however,* That those Senators who, as of January 9, 1963, were members of the Committee on Aeronautical and Space Sciences and the Committee on Government Operations—

Which I interpolate are the two minor committees now to be made major committees—

> shall be entitled to serve on three of the foregoing standing committees.

The "foregoing standing committees" referred to are the major committees. It includes all of the legislative committees of the Senate, except the Committee on the District of Columbia, the Committee on Post Office and Civil Service, and the Committee on Rules and Administration. Note that it also excepts the Joint Atomic Energy Committee, a legislative committee which, for reasons quite obscure to me, is excluded from consideration with the other legislative committees. It is said that that is because it is a joint committee with the House. But I suggest that that is a distinction without a difference. The Joint Committee on Atomic Energy is one of the most important legislative committees in the Senate. It was created by Public Law 703 of the 83d Congress, which provides:

> All bills, resolutions and other matters in the Senate or the House relating primarily to the Commission on Atomic Energy, or to the development, use, or control of atomic energy, shall be referred to the Joint Committee, whose members shall report from time to time, if they are Senate Members to the Senate, if they are House Members to the House, by bill.

Such bills are placed on the calendar and are treated like any other bills.

So it seems to me that there is no adequate reason why the Joint Atomic Energy Committee is not a major committee.

The "grandfather" clause reveals publicly a condition which has existed privately for some time, and that is that there is a class of 21 preferred Senators who are permitted to hold positions on more than 2 major committees.

To some extent this situation has existed for a number of years, but it will exist to an even greater extent from now on, if and when the "grandfather" clause becomes a part of the rules of the Senate.

Fifteen of these 21 Senators are Democrats, and 6 are Republicans. Scattered like stars on the list are the names of many Members of the Senate establishment. However, the list does contain the names of Senators who I think would deny, and correctly deny, that they are even remotely connected with the establishment, although there are not many of them.

In a moment I shall ask unanimous consent to have the list printed in the *Record,* but I cannot refrain from pointing out the very successful efforts of several Senators to advance the interests of their home States by getting on as many committees as possible.

The Senator from Nebraska [Mr. Curtis], for example, serves on the Aeronautical and Space Sciences Committee, a major committee; the Finance Committee, a major committee; the Government Operations Committee, a major committee; the Joint Committee on Atomic Energy, which is in fact if not in law one of the most important major committees of all; and, in addition, on the Rules and Administration Committee which is now a major committee, but will become a minor committee if and when the proposed change in the rules is adopted. The

Senator from Nebraska [Mr. Curtis] is in a class all by himself. No other Senator serves on five legislative committees.

My beloved friend, the senior Senator from Georgia [Mr. Russell], runs him a good second. The Senator from Georgia serves on the Aeronautical and Space Sciences Committee, the Armed Services Committee, the Appropriations Committee, and the Joint Committee on Atomic Energy; and he also serves on the Democratic steering committee and the Democratic policy committee. He is the only member of the Democratic Party except the elected leadership who serves on both the policy committee and the steering committee.

The Senator from Iowa [Mr. Hickenlooper] is up in front with the Senator from Georgia [Mr. Russell]. I commend him for his ability to serve the interests of his State by becoming a member—and, indeed, in at least one instance the ranking minority member—of very important Senate committees. He serves on the Aeronautical and Space Sciences Committee, the Agriculture and Forestry Committee, the Foreign Relations Committee, and the Joint Committee on Atomic Energy.

Mr. President, I ask unanimous consent that the list showing the committees on which these 21 Senators serve may be printed in the *Record* at this point in my remarks.

There being no objection, the list was ordered to be printed in the *Record,* as follows:

TWENTY-ONE SENATORS (15 DEMOCRATS, 6 REPUBLICANS) WITH THREE MAJOR COMMITTEES UNDER SENATE RESOLUTION 90, AS PROPOSED

ANDERSON (Democrat):[1] Interior, Space, Finance (plus Joint Atomic Energy).

CANNON (Democrat):[2] Armed Services, Space, Commerce (and Rules).

CASE (Republican): Space, Armed Services, Appropriations.

CURTIS (Republican):[1,2] Space, Finance, Government Operations (and Rules) (plus Joint Atomic Energy).

DODD (Democrat): Space, Foreign Relations, Judiciary.

ERVIN (Democrat): Armed Services, Government Operations, Judiciary.

---

[1] Five Senators with three major, plus Joint Atomic Energy Committee assignments.

[2] Two Senators with three major and one minor committee assignments.

GRUENING (Democrat): Government Operations, Interior, Public Works.

HICKENLOOPER (Republican):[1] Space, Agriculture, and Foreign Relations (plus Joint Atomic Energy).

HOLLAND (Democrat): Space, Agriculture, Appropriations.

HUMPHREY (Democrat): Appropriations, Foreign Relations, Government Operations.

JACKSON (Democrat):[1] Armed Services, Government Operations and Interior (plus Joint Atomic Energy).

JAVITS (Republican): Government Operations, Labor and Public Welfare, Banking and Currency.

MC CLELLAN (Democrat): Government Operations, Appropriations, Judiciary.

MAGNUSON (Democrat): Commerce, Space, Appropriations.

MUNDT (Republican): Foreign Relations, Appropriations, Government Operations.

MUSKIE (Democrat): Banking and Currency, Government Operations, Public Works.

RUSSELL (Democrat):[1] Space, Armed Services, Appropriations (plus Joint Atomic Energy).

SMITH (Republican): Space, Appropriations, Armed Services.

STENNIS (Democrat): Space, Appropriations, Armed Services.

SYMINGTON (Democrat): Space, Armed Services, Foreign Relations.

YOUNG of Ohio (Democrat): Space, Armed Services, Public Works.

MR. CLARK Mr. President, if these 21 Senators constitute a preferred group—and they do—then the other 79 Senators, in a sense, are second class Senators because they will be prohibited by rule XXV, if and when it is amended, from serving on more than two of these major legislative committees.

I wonder why such discrimination will occur? Is it only chance? Perhaps it is. Is it only seniority? Certainly seniority plays a part.

I urged the Democratic steering committee to eliminate the "grandfather" clause and to require all Senators who serve on both the Committee on Government Operations and the Committee on Aeronautical and Space Sciences to relinquish one of their three committees in order that more junior Senators might have an opportunity to be appointed to those committees and share the work-load of the Senate in a more equitable fashion, and also to give to their States the additional representation which membership on these important committees would give to them. I stood alone in that regard and did not, therefore, press the matter to a vote. Unless unexpected support should develop for my position over the weekend, I do not intend to fight the "grandfather" clause on the floor.

It is my recollection that in the closing decades of the 19th century the Supreme Court of the United States found the "grandfather" clauses in various southern State constitutions to be unconstitutional. I suggest that the "grandfather" clause which is about to be written into rule XXV of the Senate, if not unconstitutional—and of course the court will never pass on that, I assume—is at least inequitable and unwise. I hope that as Senators reflect on this question in the days, months, and perhaps years ahead, they will give some thought to the elimination of this grandfather clause.

I hope, also, that consideration will be given to making the Joint Committee on Atomic Energy a major committee, which in fact it is.

I note, that neither the majority leader nor the minority leader is in the Chamber, but I hope that when this question is brought to a vote on Monday, they will give us an explanation of a clause written into Senate Resolution 90 after it was printed. My understanding is—although I am not certain I am correct —that this clause was suggested by the Parliamentarian and adopted by the majority leader and minority leader at his suggestion.

After reciting the clause as I read it previously, providing that all Senators who, as of January 9, 1963, were members of two formerly minor committees, now to be made major committees, shall be entitled to serve on three of the foregoing standing committees, the resolution provides that "no Senator shall serve on more than one of the following committees, as well as any Senator who is appointed temporarily to fill any vacancy arising out of this proviso."

What that means, I do not know. I hope we shall be told how "temporary" that is. I presume it is an expansion of the grandfather clause to take in other Senators who are not now members of those two committees, but who might subsequently be made members of those committees, namely, the Government

Operations and Space Committees, by reason of death or resignation of present members.

If so, the key word is "temporarily." If there is some other and more ulterior purpose, one might think it means that the grandfather clause would continue indefinitely and that vacancies as they arose on these two committees might be filled by Senators who would not have to give up any of the other committees.

No doubt an adequate explanation of this clause will be forthcoming on Monday.

OTHER RULES CHANGE PROPOSALS

I turn now, Mr. President, to another matter, closely allied with that which I have been discussing. The problem of the size, composition, ratio, and selection of members of committees is a very important one, but this is only one matter out of many with respect to which drastic need exists to modernize and streamline the Senate rules. As to any of the other proposed methods to modernize and streamline the Senate, the bipartisan Senate establishment has set its face rigorously against change.

I have introduced and have pending 15 proposed changes in the present rules of the Senate, all intended to democratize Senate action, all intended to expedite Senate action, all intended to make it easier for the program of the President to receive fair and prompt consideration, all intended to let the Senate perform its constitutional duties more effectively.

I now submit again, as I did with Congresswoman Green of Oregon last year, a 16th proposed change, in the form of a concurrent resolution which would provide for the face lifting and streamlining of the *Congressional Record;* and ask unanimous consent that the proposed concurrent resolution may be referred to the Committee on Rules and Administration, and I ask that its text be printed in the *Record* at this point in my remarks.

The PRESIDING OFFICER The concurrent resolution will be received and appropriately referred; and, without objection, the concurrent resolution will be printed in the *Record.*

The concurrent resolution (S. Con. Res. 22) submitted by

Mr. Clark, was referred to the Committee on Rules and Administration, as follows:

> Whereas the *Congressional Record* is established as substantially a verbatim report of proceedings of both Houses of the Congress; and
>
> Whereas Congress is the staging area for the discussion and resolution of the major national issues confronting the United States; and
>
> Whereas this "national dialog" reaches a climax in the passage or the defeat of legislation; and
>
> Whereas thousands among the leaders of our country in both public and private stations depend upon the *Congressional Record* for details of these dialogs: Therefore be it
>
> *Resolved by the Senate (the House of Representatives concurring),* That the Joint Committee on Printing, which is assigned control and supervision of the *Record* under sections 181 and 182 of chapter 6, title 44, United States Code, conduct a study of the *Congressional Record* with a view to improving its format, index, typography, organization of materials, and other aspects relevant to such a study; and be it further
>
> *Resolved,* That the Joint Committee on Printing, if it deems it provident, shall call upon experts in the communications media and possibly public spirited citizens, such as civic leaders, Government officials, and scholars, to sit as an advisory committee in order to render such help as may be needed; and be it further
>
> *Resolved,* That the Joint Committee on Printing shall, if it deems it advisable, be empowered to incur whatever expenditures are necessary to the proper carrying out of this study, but that in no event shall the sum exceed the amount of $50,000; and be it further
>
> *Resolved,* That the joint committee shall report its findings to the Congress within one year after date of passage of this concurrent resolution.

MR. CLARK   Mr. President, when I submitted a similar resolution last year I expressed the hope that a part of the face lifting of the *Congressional Record* would provide amply for the printing of cartoons, so the *Record* could be enlivened and we could have something in format not unlike the publication which so many of my colleagues, but not I, admire so extravagantly— *Life,* that journal of plutocratic opinion.

I am particularly unhappy that we cannot have cartoons printed in the *Record* now. One of the most enlightened and amusing cartoons in history appeared in the *Washington Post* this morning. I hope my colleagues and others who read the

"What Does He Think This Is — A Legislative Body?"

"What Does He Think This Is——A Legislative Body?"
—Herblock in the *Washington Post*

Record will obtain access to the editorial page of the *Washington Post* of this morning and have a good chuckle over that cartoon. I shall say nothing further about it.

These proposed rule changes are presently languishing in the Committee on Rules and Administration, to which I have just been assigned, and where I shall do my best to have them reported favorably, or, if not favorably, at least unfavorably, so that the Senate can act on them. I am confident there will be a strong minority report, if not majority report, in support of some, if not all, of the following proposals:

First, to have a Joint Committee on the Organization of Congress, a new La Follette-Monroney committee. This proposal has 32 sponsors. I should say it might have some chance of success.

Second, a new Senate rule on selection of conferees, providing that a majority of Senate Members appointed to represent the Senate on conference committees would have to be chosen from those who had indicated by their votes their acquiescence in those provisions of the bills passed by the Senate with which the House was in disagreement.

Third, a rule which would permit Senate committees to sit while the Senate was in session unless a majority of the Senate, on a vote without debate, should determine otherwise.

My good friend the senior Senator from Idaho [Mr. Church] has advised me he will soon propose—I hope with the support of the majority leader—a new Senate order of business. This order would provide that until the hour of 2 o'clock each day Senate committees could meet while the Senate was in session; that until the hour of 2 o'clock each day Senators could talk on any subject which came into their heads; there would be a morning hour; perhaps there would be a recess for lunch so that Senators could meet their obligations to their constituents and to others; then the Senate would reassemble in at 2 o'clock and there would be 4 hours of continuous germane debate on the pending business.

This latter proposal is jointly sponsored by the senior Senator from Rhode Island [Mr. Pastore] and my good friend from Idaho [Mr. Church]. I believe a large number of other Senators concur in the suggestion.

While it is not the way I would have done it, Mr. President, it is so much better than our present procedure that I would be happy to join in this salutory reform in our rules and procedures if there were any chance of success.

Clearly, it is a deterrent to the orderly conduct of business to permit nongermane debate—really, hardly ever debate, although sometimes, but merely nongermane speeches—which take the time of the Senate and make it impossible to expedite the conduct of business.

My fourth rule change deals with the subject of germaneness.

Fifth, I would provide that insertions in the *Record* might be made upon request without Senators having to read texts in full. Speeches might be put in the *Record* without the necessity of reading them in full, and printed in large type. This would do away with the the hypocritical practice of reading the first and last paragraphs of a long speech, anticipating that it will be printed in full and in large type in the *Record* to look as though it had been delivered to a rapt audience of the entire Senate and to rapt and breathless occupants of the galleries.

If one looks around the Chamber of the Senate now, he will see what might be called normal Senate attendance. The very able junior Senator from Ohio [Mr. Young] is waiting to make his speech. In the chair at present is a very able freshman Senator [Mr. McIntyre]. In addition, I am present, and there is also present the new Senator from New Mexico [Mr. Mechem], who is holding down, with great ability and some persistence, the seat of the minority leader, who, I presume, is off on other business which he considers more important than listening again to the senior Senator from Pennsylvania on a subject with respect to which the distinguished minority leader does not find himself in agreement with the views of the senior Senator from Pennsylvania.

The next proposed rule would change the jurisdiction of committees so as to make a more equitable distribution of the business of the Senate and minimize to some extent the heavy overburden of business presently referred to the Committee on Finance, the Committee on Foreign Relations, and the Committee on Commerce.

My eighth change would place an age limit on holding committee chairmanships. This, I believe, is an extremely salutary reform. This is the same limit which Congress places on judges of our Federal court and which has induced retirement at the age of 70 in many a case. I might point out that there is an inducement in the judiciary to retire at 70 in the form of an enhanced pension. I would be very glad to vote for a similar provision with respect to chairmen of Senate committees. As in the case of judges, of course, I would not propose that they withdraw from service on the committee at 70 but merely cease operating as chairmen.

My ninth proposed rule change would provide that chairmen of all standing committees should be chosen by secret ballot of a majority of the entire committee at the beginning of each new Congress.

My 10th proposed change would create a committee bill of rights, and would provide that within each committee a majority of its members could be authorized to convene meetings, call up bills for consideration, and terminate debate after reasonable discussion of issues in executive session, so that the business of the committee could not be delayed and sometimes prevented from coming to a vote by action of the chairman or a minority of the committee.

My 11th change would be to eliminate the requirement that it takes unanimous consent to dispense with the reading of the Journal. In the 8-plus years that I have been in the Senate, I recall only one occasion when the dispensing with the reading of the Journal was objected to for any purpose other than delay. There was one occasion when a Senator felt that he did not believe the Journal correctly represented his point of view. That matter was disposed of in short order. On a half dozen other occasions the purpose of objecting to dispensing with the reading of the Journal was purely for the purpose of delay or, when I did it—and I did it several times—to demonstrate the absurdity of the rule.

The 12th proposed change would rewrite the morning hour rule, which is now never followed. I suggest it should be rewritten to conform with the present practice. I would hope that the rule would also be rewritten in connection with the proposed reform under the rule which the Senator from Idaho [Mr. Church] and the Senator from Rhode Island [Mr. Pastore] have in mind. My 13th, 14th, and 15th proposals are Senate Resolutions 91, 92, and 93, which will be before the Senate on Monday.

I do not know that the Senate will have a yea-and-nay vote on any or all of the resolutions, but it may. They would provide for increasing the membership of the Appropriations Committee from 27 to 29, the Finance Committee from 17 to 21, and the Foreign Relations Committee from 17 to 21. The ratio would be 19 Democrats and 10 Republicans on the Appropriations Committee, 14 Democrats and 7 Republicans on the Finance Committee, and 14 Democrats and 7 Republicans on the Foreign Relations Committee.

RECOMMENDATIONS

I would like to summarize the recommendations which flow from this discussion of the Senate establishment. First, I believe the steering committee of the Democratic conference should be reorganized. The conference has decided not to increase its size from 15 to 19 or from 15 to 17. I consider myself bound by that vote for the present session of Congress, unless and until the majority leader should change his mind—and I hope he will—and bring us back into conference to change the size of the committee. I am confident that at any time the Senate majority leader makes that decision, the size of the committee will be changed as he requests. He has the votes to do it.

With all due deference to the majority leader, who has been kindness itself to me ever since I came to the Senate, and particularly has been kind indeed in connection with this most unpopular speech which I am about to conclude, I must say that he has a commitment to the Democratic conference, in my opinion, to see that the steering committee of the Democratic Party adequately reflects both the geography and the ideology of the members of the Democratic conference. That commitment was made in 1961. It was made again in 1963. It has not been carried out.

If it is determined not to seek an increase in the size of the steering committee, then there is another very simple way in which the same result can be achieved, and that is to have two of my fine southern friends resign from the committee, to permit in their place two additional Kennedy Democrats to be placed on the committee from either the Middle West—and certainly one of them should come from there—or from the Mountain or Western States, or from the Atlantic Seaboard States, which have so heavy a share of the population of the United States.

I certainly would not want to suggest who should resign, but with my tongue in cheek I would suggest that the fairest way might be to have the junior southern Senators on the committee resign. However, I say that in a somewhat lighter fashion, because I have no doubt that these gentlemen would decide this matter for themselves and would not welcome any particular advice from me.

I point out that both Senators from Florida are on that committee, and I suggest that is not a very equitable situation.

Therefore, my first recommendation would be to reconstitute the steering committee.

My second recommendation would be to increase the size of the Committee on Appropriations, the Finance Committee, and the Foreign Relations Committee, so that Senators passed over in committee assignments last week could get their just due, and so that the program of the President might get its fair and prompt attention.

My third recommendation would be that the Senate act promptly in considering the changes in the rules which I have just discussed.

CONCLUSIONS

Mr. President, why all this fuss? Why should I have taken the time of the Senate on 3 separate days to raise these matters? The first reason is that procedure is the heart of justice. Without just procedure, whether it be due process of law, enshrined in the 5th and 14th amendments to the Constitution, or whether it be the rules, customs, manners, and traditions of the Senate, procedure is the heart of justice. We are operating today under rules, procedures, customs, and traditions which are unjust, unfair, and undemocratic.

So while I sympathize with the majority leader when he suggests that we should get to the Senate business, I say there is no more important Senate business than assuring, at the beginning of a session, that the procedures of the Senate are just.

There appears on the Calendar Senate Resolution 9, which is supported by 56 Senators and is opposed by that Senate Establishment, bipartisan in nature, which refuses to allow the Senate to act on a matter of justice, of equity, of democracy, and of fairness, for which 56 of its Members plead. This problem will be on the conscience of the Senate until a vote is allowed on Senate Resolution 9.

Again and again during this session, those 56 Senators will call to the attention of the southern bloc and of their Republican colleagues that "There, on your consciences as Senators of the United States, lies the heavy charge that you will not permit the Senate to act on a resolution of importance to its internal government, to its fairness, to its justice, when a clear majority of the Senate, 56 out of 100, have put themselves on the record by their votes and by their pairs to change this rule."

Mr. President, Carthage must be destroyed. There must be a vote on Senate Resolution 9. There is no justice, there is no equity in forbidding a vote because of the outmoded method of unlimited debate. So the principal reason for all this fuss is, as I say, that procedure is the heart of justice.

Another reason, in all candor, is that the Senate has no legislative business to transact. Why should we not discuss questions of procedure until measures of legislative importance, on which we can act, are on the calendar? The only important item on the calendar today is Senate Resolution 9; and that is the only legislative business which the Senate establishment does not want us to dispose of. It is not we—the Kennedy men, the liberals, the independent and forward-looking Republicans—who are holding up the conduct of Senate business; it is the Senate establishment which will not let us vote on the only measure of any importance which is on the calendar, and which is ready for action.

So I close, as I began, with the plea to my colleagues to make a beginning in the modernization of the Senate and its procedures; to make a beginning in the elimination of control by a small group of bipartisan Senators, fine persons, I say at the end, as I said when I began—friends of mine they have been in the past, friends of mine I hope they will continue to be in the future—who are committed to the status quo, who seem to be committed to sectional rule; who, with all due deference, I suggest—and I do defer to those fine and honorable Senators— have an unawareness of the modern world and of the dangers confronting us from a resourceful antagonist overseas, whose government is able to act in an instant; an unawareness of the danger that our Government will not be able to act in a crisis because the Senate of the United States has rendered itself, by its ancient, archaic, and obsolete rules unable to act when its majority is ready for action.

In the end, the Republic is in jeopardy. Perhaps not today, perhaps not tomorrow, but who knows when? It is later than we think. The Senate should bring itself up to the needs and the challenges of the seventh decade of the twentieth century.

Mr. President, I yield the floor.

MR. DOUGLAS   Mr. President, while I have been listening to the Senator from Pennsylvania [Mr. Clark] for the past 3 days, and have been studying his remarks in the *Congressional Record* each morning closely, I have been debating with myself whether I should seek recognition from the Presiding Officer to discuss the points which he has brought out.

I am well aware that to speak on this subject is not popular; that it does not advance one in the assignment of positions; and that it tends to be resented by many who occupy influential positions in the Senate and in the country.

Nevertheless, I felt that it was my duty to indicate that the Senator from Pennsylvania did not stand alone in what he said, and that some indication should be given, through the *Congressional Record,* that there are some—and I believe many—of us who believe in the basic positions which he has been advancing.

Let me say at the very beginning that I have no personal complaints to make so far as my own treatment is concerned. I am a member of two important committees, the Banking and Currency Committee, of which I have been a member ever since I first came to the Senate more than 14 years ago, and the Finance Committee, which I tried to get on for a number of years and had some difficulty in making, but to which I was finally assigned. I am also a member of the Joint Economic Committee.

So I want to make it clear that I have absolutely no complaint about the way I have been assigned to committees, nor have I any complaint whatsoever about the way I have been treated by those who hold different opinions from mine on public policy. Furthermore, I have no animus toward those who are in control of the party senatorial policy. I do not question their motives. I think they are conscientious, according to their lights, and that they have in many ways estimable qualities which deserve recognition.

Nevertheless, the Senator from Pennsylvania has put his finger on one of the weaknesses of our party and one of the weaknesses of the Senate.

The Democratic Party wins its presidential elections by the votes of the great industrial States. It wins those elections on platforms which are believed in by the voters and which pledge to carry out legislative programs which will be in the interest of the great masses of the American people; namely, the wage earners, the small farmers, the white-collar workers, the small businessmen, the housewives, and the consumers. That is how we win our presidential elections. Then the Congress convenes, and we are not able to pass any considerable portion of the program upon which we have gone to the country, and we find that the machinery of the Senate, and I think largely of the House, is in the hands of those who fundamentally do not believe in the program by which the presidential election was won and for which the great mass of voters in the country cast their ballots.

We all know this to be a fact. No one can be around this body for 2 or 3 years—indeed, less than that—without knowing it to be the case. No one can be around here for any space of time without knowing that the combination against such a program operates from both sides of the aisle; that what we have is really a bipartisan alliance, a coalition which is basically opposed to the platform of the Democratic Party.

Many of us have been reading the book *The Deadlock of Democracy* by James Burns, in which I think he correctly states that there are four parties. Even though I think his classification is not precisely accurate, there are four parties. There are the liberal and progressive Democrats, the conservative Democrats, the conservative Republicans, and the liberal Republicans—a small but gallant band. The two center groups, conservative Democrats and conservative Republicans, work in very close alliance with each other, dominate the major committees, control the procedures of the Senate, and in the main stymie the legislation for which the presidential candidate of the Democratic Party has gone to the country.

There is no use, to my mind, in denying these facts, but apparently it is regarded as bad form to call attention to them. I am reminded of the story in Hans Christian Andersen's "Fairy Tales," about the emperor who had a suit of clothes supposedly woven for him which was in reality nonexistent. He paraded in this suit of clothes. Others were expected to admire the suit of clothes. Finally, a very naive boy said, "The emperor has no clothes." Then the illusion was punctured and the people saw the king in his full nakedness. The reluctance of some to discuss the facts of the organization of the Senate is similar to the reluctance to admit that the emperor had no clothes.

Consider the committee chairmanships. Of 14 major chairmen, 10 come from the Southern States, 2 from the Southwestern States, and 2 from States in other parts of the country.

I refer to the bipartisan coalition—I suppose the Senator from Pennsylvania would call it the senatorial establishment—and its followers. I suppose the author of *The Citadel* would call it the club. They mean the same thing and largely refer to the same persons. They control the Senate.

I personally believe the result of permitting the coalition's dominance to continue has been that we have not moved forward in the field of legislation as rapidly as we should have done. I also feel, as a Democrat, that it is of increasing disadvantage to the party in making an appeal to the country, because people are properly saying, "You campaign on these platforms, but you do not or cannot put them into effect when we elect you."

Therefore, the bipartisan alliance, which really carries out the Republican platform, operates against Democratic senatorial and congressional candidates from the North and the West, operates against our presidential candidate, and is indeed an albatross around the neck of the Democratic Party.

Yet we are not supposed to talk about it because we might offend someone or might indicate that matters are decided in a different way from the way they are discussed in public. In short, we should not call attention to the nakedness of the emperor.

However, I happen to be one who believes that the truth in these matters is extremely important and that to recognize the facts is the first step toward cure. We all know it is so in the field of medicine. Diagnosis comes first; cure comes second. As long as one denies he is ill, as long as he believes everything is fine, he will not take steps to cure the situation. Not until evidence piles up, crippling symptoms appear, and real sickness develops are corrective measures adopted.

As I explained the other day, I was put on the steering committee, to my surprise, only 5 minutes before I had to go to Illinois. I left my proxy with the Senator from Pennsylvania. He cast that proxy for me in a manner which would increase the strength of the section of the Democratic Party which believes in the national platform and supports basically the program which the President is trying to put into effect.

Two days ago, when I read of some of the choices which were made, and some of the men who were denied positions, I raised the question as to whether there was any pattern in the decisions which were made, whether this was all "happenstance" and confusion, or whether a pattern developed, without going into the matter of motive in the slightest.

The Senator from Pennsylvania had a study made, which he put into the *Record* of yesterday, and which has been twice summarized. I believe it is worthy of repetition. I have checked his study against the worksheets of committee assignments and I believe it to be wholly accurate.

Eight nonfreshman Senators who opposed a rules change submitted eligible bids for new committee assignments. Seven of them received new committee assignments. Six got the assignments that represented their first choice. They did very well. Fourteen nonfreshman Senators who supported a rules change applied for new committee assignments. Only one Senator of the group, the Senator from Montana [Mr. Mansfield], got the committee of his first choice. Four others got some minor assignments.

I know that statistical correlation is not necessarily proof of causation. However, this coincidence is really striking; and certainly it is true that a mathematical pattern developed in connection with these assignments. That mathematical pattern shows something which the Senator from Pennsylvania did not mention but which I believe I should mention.

It shows clearly that the Democratic steering committee exercises discretion in awarding new assignments to nonfreshman Senators in such a way that a large majority of those who had favored a rules change were disappointed, and a large majority of those who opposed a rules change were given their requested assignments. This is the pattern. I defy anyone to draw any different conclusions from it.

As I say, in accordance with not only the rules of the Senate, but also the practices of the Senate, I do not make any charge as to motive. I merely say that that is what happened. That is what has tended to happen year after year.

The result of this decision, both on the numbers to be included on the Finance Committee—which I regard as the most crucial decision made—and on the assignment of individual Senators, has been such as to put the President's program in grave jeopardy.

For about 7 years I have been a member of the Finance Committee. I like my colleagues on the committee. I have respect for the chairman of the committee, who has great personal integrity.

However, for years in my judgment this committee has not supported the national program of the Democratic Party. Unless there is a change in the position of the committee or a change in the opinions of this particular committee, it is going to be extremely difficult to carry out the program of the Democratic Party so far as at least two important measures are concerned, namely, the tax bill, and the hospital and nursing care for the aged bill, which was introduced today. If we fail to pass these bills in any meaningful form, it will be in part due to the position of the Finance Committee. That committee, incidentally, violates the proportion which exists in the Senate. The proportion between Democrats and Republicans in the Senate is slightly better than 2 to 1. The proportion on the Finance Committee is 11 to 6. In years past a sufficient number of Democrats, high ranking members, have almost always sided with the Republicans, so that in effect the party of the President, the party of the national platform, was in a decided minority, and the committee was not able to report bills in the fashion indicated.

Much the same thing has been true in the Committee on the Judiciary. While I do not complain about anything that has happened to me—indeed I have no grounds for complaint—I feel that I ought to enter an objection to certain decisions which were made adverse to Senators who have tried to carry out the program of the Democratic National Party.

I should like to mention only three of these Senators. I could mention more. However, I wish to start with the Senator from North Dakota [Mr. Burdick], who twice has sought a seat on the Committee on the Judiciary and twice has been passed over.

In this instance I know he was passed over again in favor of Senators with much less seniority. I do not complain about the character of the men who were selected. I merely say that here is a Senator from North Dakota, a good lawyer, one of the best lawyers in the Northwest, the son of the beloved Usher L. Burdick, who for many years was a Member of the House, a man who, though he does not have more than a handful of Negroes in his State, and who has always voted for civil rights legislation.

By his qualities, by his record, he abundantly deserves being placed on the Judiciary Committee. Yet he has been twice passed over.

I should like to mention another Senator, the Senator from Utah [Mr. Moss], one of the finest men in the Senate—quiet, unobtrusive, modest, but a man who has tremendous courage and great integrity. I could tell many stories about Frank Moss, to indicate the quality of the man, but for confidential reasons, I shall not do so. He also comes from a State which has almost no Negroes in it, but he has always voted for civil rights legislation.

These two men get no political gains from the position they take on civil rights, or from the position which they take in believing that sometimes the Senate should be allowed to vote on certain measures. There is, in well-known parlance, no political "moxie" attached to what they do. They take the position they do as a matter of conscience. They cannot be accused of following anything but their conscience in their actions.

Men like that should be rewarded, not punished, because in political life conscience tends to be eroded. It needs to be fostered, not discouraged. The attitude of these men is above and beyond praise. It is not popular for them to take the position they take. It is not popular for anyone to take that position, but especially it is not popular for them to take it.

Yet for reasons of conscience they do what they do. They suffer for it. The only conclusion which the general public can draw— I do not say that I draw it—the only conclusion which the general public can draw, is that there is a connection between the stand which they take and the punishment which they receive. Others, who look on and see what happens to these men, will have the feeling that if they become independent and take this position, they are likely to experience the same results. It is only necessary to punish a few men in order to deter others. That is the secret of intimidation. If a few are punished, that punishment operates automatically upon others.

I could go on. I believe that the senior Senator from Wisconsin [Mr. Proxmire] should have received an assignment either to the Committee on Finance or the Committee on Appropriations. He was entitled to one or the other of those assignments on the basis of seniority. Certainly he is entitled to one or the other of those positions on the basis of knowledge or ability. I do not always agree with him on everything. I favor a tax cut under the present economic situation. The senior Senator from Wisconsin does not favor a tax cut. But he knows what he is talking about. He never twists the facts. He works hard. He is a man of great integrity. I regard him as one of the most valuable Members of this body. The way in which he scrutinizes appropriation bills commands my esteem. As a battle-scarred veteran of this effort I thank Heaven there is someone young, vigorous, and strong who is doing this work. In my judgment, the senior Senator from Wisconsin has saved the taxpayers of the Nation a great deal of money. He should have been assigned either to the Committee on Appropriations or to the Committee on Finance. I tended to favor him for the Committee on Finance.

There were other failures to assign to committees which may not have been so conspicuous as the cases which I have cited, but which, nonetheless, occurred. The junior Senator from California [Mr. Engle], a Democrat who adopts a national point of view, sought assignment to the Committee on Appropriations, but he was not so assigned.

The junior Senator from Michigan [Mr. Hart] was passed over for his first and second choices, the Committee on Appropriations and the Committee on Armed Services. He is one of the most conscientious Members of Congress. He also is a strong defender of civil rights and of the national program of the Democratic Party. But he was relegated to a less important committee; namely, the Committee on Commerce.

The junior Senator from Ohio [Mr. Young] was passed over. He had served on the House Committee on Ways and Means and was abundantly qualified for the Committee on Finance.

The senior Senator from Pennsylvania [Mr. Clark] in past years was passed over for assignment to the Committee on Foreign Relations in favor of those having less seniority.

So I submit that a pattern tends to emerge, in which one takes an occupational risk, in all probability, by voting for a change in the cloture rule, by voting for civil rights, by voting to reduce the depletion allowance, and, in general, by following the national platform of the Democratic Party. This punishment is meted out by one's own party associates. It is not a way to make the party in Congress responsive to the platform upon which we run and upon which we seek votes.

Like many other Senators, I have been reading the political history of Congress during the years immediately preceding the Civil War. At that time the Democratic Party was divided between the northern Democrats, who, in the main, believed in freedom, and the southern Democrats, who believed in slavery and in its extension.

The southern Democrats controlled the political organization of the party in the Senate and the House. They insisted on a rigid control of the party in their interest, and they drove out of the Democratic Party some of its fine spirits, perhaps its best spirits, in the North. We sometimes forget that Salmon P. Chase started out in life as a Democrat. He was a Democrat in the U.S. Senate. We forget that Lyman Trumbull, of my State, was a Democrat until the Kansas-Nebraska Act was passed. He could not stomach it any longer, and he had to leave.

Gideon Welles was an antislavery Democrat of the North. There was a large group of such men. But the South insisted on its proslavery policy and drove those men out of the Democratic Party. They found their way into the Republican Party. And for the following 52 years, the Democratic Party remained out of power, with the exception of the two administrations of Grover Cleveland.

I am not suggesting that the situation today is precisely analogous. I am not suggesting that our southern friends wish to eliminate the 13th amendment and to restore slavery. I can say, however, that in the main they are determined to ignore the 14th and 15th amendments to the Constitution—not all of them, but the majority of them. I regard the 14th and 15th amendments to the Constitution as integral portions of the Constitution, just as much as any other section of the Constitution. Dominant white opinion in the South is not willing to give the Negro those basic rights over which the Civil War was fought and won.

I personally believe that Congress should take advantage of the section in each of those amendments which gives to Congress the power to pass legislation to make those amendments effective. I do not regard the 14th and 15th amendments as mere window dressing, as mere language of high ideals useful to make people feel good but which is devoid of reality. I think they are meant as guidelines to action.

It remains to be seen whether we will be permitted to make the 14th and 15th amendments effective. If we are not, I am confident it will not be good for the country, and it will not be good for the Democratic Party.

Who were the northerners whom the South permitted in the days before the Civil War to take some share in the leadership of the Democratic Party? They were called "doughfaces." A "doughface" was defined as a northern man with southern principles. So from 1852 to 1862 the country had two "doughface" Presidents—Franklin Pierce, who graduated from my college, and was one of the poorest Presidents the country ever had; and James Buchanan, another "doughface." They nearly brought the country to ruin. And there were "doughfaces" in the Senate and in the House. Perhaps the most injurious of them was Jesse B. Bright, of Indiana, who favored the extension of slavery into the Territories. Stephen A. Douglas, whose seat I now occupy, hesitated for a long time before deciding whether he would be a "doughface." But finally, in 1857 and 1858, he had the manhood to refuse to go along with the program which would have forced the extension of slavery into the Territories. He paid for that by being defeated in his bid for his party's nomination for President of the United States in 1860; and the party paid for it by its split.

Of course, there is another difference between the situation today and the situation in the days preceding the Civil War; it is that the national leaders of our party are not "doughfaces." Presidents Roosevelt, Truman, and Kennedy have, in the main, been leaders of the liberal wing of our party—a party which believes we should stand for human rights, and that the Government is intended to better the condition of the average man and the average woman. They are not always as militant in supporting these principles as we might like them to be; but we realize the political difficulties they encounter. They know they have to deal with the party structure in the Senate and in the House. They do not wish to engage in battles which, in the short run, will be lost. But the restraints which operate upon a

President need not, and in my judgment should not, operate on Members of the Senate and Members of the House. Some of the legislation we favor may be "derailed"; some reprisals may occur. But in the main we have the obligation to our party and to the country to speak out, because, frankly, this is an intolerable situation. It is intolerable for us to win national elections, but be unable to carry the program into effect. It is intolerable to have the congressional leaders of our party in the main oppose the program of the party, or, if they do not openly oppose it, support those who do oppose it. The people of this Nation are not fools. They can see through what is happening. It was only necessary for that one child to say, "The emperor has no clothes on," for people to realize that that was so. In medieval days, in the days of absolute monarchies, the only man who was permitted to tell the truth was the court fool. That is the entire basis of Erasmus' famous book "In Praise of Folly." Only folly was permitted to be wise. The court fool could tell the truth, because if he did, others could always say, "Well, he is just the fool."

Mr. President, I think the party and the Senate need a few people who will say, "The emperor has no clothes on," and who will state the truth.

It is not popular to do that. The Senator from Pennsylvania [Mr. Clark] took great risks by making the speech he made. He can always be accused of "sour grapes," and can be told, "The legislation you favor will not go through. The dam your constituents want will not be built. The river improvements your constituents want will not be made." But the Senator from Pennsylvania felt that he must speak out, and I think he has performed a very valuable service.

He did not speak to a crowded Senate; and I am not speaking to a crowded Senate, either, exactly. Very few of the lords of the press are now in the Press Gallery. But our words will appear in the *Congressional Record*, which some people read; and voices in this country are not entirely muffled.

Mr. President, I wish to say, in all kindness, that the Democratic Party is not served by putting the congressional structure of the party in opposition to its platform. The Democratic Party is not served by attempting to deny the existence of palpable truths. The Democratic Party is not served when Senators such as the Senator from Utah [Mr. Moss], the Senator from North Dakota [Mr. Burdick], the Senator from Wisconsin [Mr. Proxmire], the Senator from Michigan [Mr. Hart], the Senator from Ohio [Mr. Young], and the Senator from California [Mr. Engle] are discriminated against; nor is the Democratic Party served when Senators who go along with the bipartisan coalition are rewarded. Jesse Bright does not cut a very glorious figure in the history of the U.S. Senate. Salmon Chase as a Senator cuts a very good figure. I do not approve of everything he did afterwards; but he was a heroic Senator.

Unless we put more vitality into the congressional work of our party, it will be very hard to go before the voters in 1964 and urge them to vote for the party. The tragedy is that in 1964, of the 24 now sitting Democratic Senators who then will be running for reelection, 21 come from the North and from the West, and, in the main, represent the progressive wing or the liberal wing of the party; they may pay with their political lives for the sins of others.

Sometimes, Mr. President, in my sardonic moments, I wonder whether this is also a part of the plan—to discredit the party, to defeat the Senators from the North and the Senators from the West who otherwise might threaten the supremacy of the bipartisan alliance, and then to emerge with an even tighter control over the Senate than before, with the bipartisan coalition swollen in numbers and the liberal opposition diminished.

It will be very interesting to watch the developments during the coming 6 or 7 months that Congress will probably be in session. I hope that the program of the President will not be derailed, but I very much fear that it will be derailed by the decisions which have already been made as to the organization of the committees. That is why I intend to vote with the Senator from Pennsylvania [Mr. Clark], even if his voice and mine are the only voices raised on the floor of the Senate when the roll is called.

The Senator has helped to ring a firebell in the night which I hope will awaken many people in the country to a realization of what they dimly suspected, but which should not stand revealed. He has given to the coalition the somewhat flossy name of "The Establishment." I suppose that is a fairly good term. We could call it "The Establishment, "The Club," "The Bipartisan Coalition," or anything else, but it is two wings of the same bird, and those wings move in unison except, as I have said, for the small but gallant band of liberal Republicans on the other side of the aisle and except for the majority of the Democrats on this side of the aisle.

The tragedy is that we cannot seem to get together. The tragedy is that the overwhelming majority of Republicans and a minority of the majority are ensconced in the seats of power, entrenched behind the rules of the Senate, able to overawe some of the swing votes, and in general to have their will. These are issues which should be discussed.

I commend the Senator from Pennsylvania for raising the question. I felt that to remain silent would be in a sense to desert him, and that he needed support. While I wish that others would come forward, they will have their opportunity next Monday.

Mr. President, I yield the floor.

February 25, 1963

MR. CLARK   Mr. President, I yield myself as much of the time remaining to me as I may require.

On Tuesday, Wednesday, and Thursday of last week I undertook to make my case on the floor of the Senate with respect to the need to change the size of three Senate committees, in order to enable Senators who support, in general, the program of the President, and who, in particular, were denied seats on these committees, to which, in my opinion, in equity and justice they were entitled, to join those committees.

I shall now very briefly summarize the case I attempted to make.

My proposal, which is pending, is to increase the size of the Finance Committee from 17—consisting of 11 Democrats and 6 Republicans—to 21, 14 Democrats and 7 Republicans. I believe this change to be highly desirable, for three reasons:

First, to bring the ratio between the Republican members and the Democratic members more nearly into line with the more than 2-to-1 majority which the Democrats presently have in the Senate—that is to say, 67 Democratic Senators and 33 Republican Senators.

Mr. President, what valid excuse can there be for leaving the ratio on the Finance Committee 11 to 6, or substantially less than 2 to 1? This committee is one of the most important of the Senate's committees. It will have before it most important proposals recommended by the President. The committee presently is controlled—as was so well pointed out by the Senator from Illinois [Mr. Douglas]—by a conservative coalition composed of southern Democratic Senators and western and northern Republican Senators, so that it does not represent the will of the majority of the Senate, nor will it, in my opinion, honest and able though each of these Senators is. I do not challenge the integrity of any Senator, nor do I challenge the sincerity of any Senator's economic views, but this committee does not represent the country or the majority of the Senate. For that reason, to maintain the present ratio with the present membership of that committee is, in my opinion, unsound and unwise.

My second reason is to make additional seats available to Senators who are entitled to them on the basis of their records in the Senate—whether by seniority or otherwise. Seniority was ignored 9 times in the assignments made by members of the Democratic steering committee, who themselves rule by seniority. Yet, Mr. President, when it seemed to them desirable to ignore seniority, they did so.

I do not challenge the motivation or impugn the good faith of anyone. All I say is that those who live by seniority should be prepared to die by it, if as a result their own position is going to be adversely affected. I suggest they should allow others to live by the same rule which they have so often invoked in support of their own position.

Let me say that, on other occasions, the size of the Finance Committee has been substantially larger than it presently is— and, indeed, larger than my proposal would make it. As recently as 1937, the Finance Committee consisted of 21 members—in other words, the same size I now propose to make it. So in this body, so devoted to precedent, there is excellent precedent for changing the size of the Finance Committee.

My third reason is to open the committee's membership to Senators who will support the programs of the President, particularly his programs with respect to taxes and medicare. I believe the power of the Executive should be increased to the extent necessary to make it possible for the legislature to give the Executive fair consideration of all measures which the Executive sends to the legislature—in short, Mr. President, that, in effect, the President should be entitled to a hearing on all the bills he favors before the appropriate committees, and before committees which properly represent the membership of the Senate, and whose membership is not based solely and alone upon the power of such a coalition as that referred to to control these important committees.

The Senate establishment opposed this proposed change. If the Senate establishment wins—and I am under no illusion in regard to this matter—I submit that the present sterile, ultraconservative control of the Finance Committee will be continued, and that the programs of the President will be crippled, if not actually destroyed.

Mr. President, let me ask how much time remains available to me?

The PRESIDING OFFICER   Ten minutes.

MR. CLARK   Mr. President, the great historian, Arnold J. Toynbee, in his massive study of history, has pointed out that a civilization advances when it is under the control of a creative minority, and that civilization decays when the minority—which to date has controlled all civilizations, and, indeed, controls ours today—is not creative, but merely is dominant, when it supports the status quo, when it is intent only on preserving power, not on advancing a forward-looking civilization, which must advance with its time.

Mr. President, I submit that today there is in the Senate a creative majority which must sooner or later wrest control from the dominant minority, if the Senate is to play its proper constitutional part in our Government's efforts to keep America moving forward in a world of change and crisis. I submit that the Senate cannot afford to stand still while every other governmental institution in the world is moving ahead to meet the challenges of our time.

Something has been said about "packing" a committee. I have said before, and I repeat now, that neither I nor any of the Senators who support the position I take is attempting to engage in a "packing" movement. This is an effort to "unstack" the committee, which presently is "stacked" against the President's supporters in the Senate.

I hope Senators will vote against keeping the clock turned back to suit the wishes of a small minority which is out of touch with the facts of modern life.

Mr. President, this controversy may seem to some to be a mere haggle over procedure. But I submit that procedure is the heart of liberty and the heart of freedom; and I submit that until the Senate frees itself from the outmoded and archaic procedures under which it is governed, there can be little hope for the enactment of a meaningful legislative program.

I call the attention of Senators and the attention of the press and the attention of the public generally to what I regard as a very pertinent quotation from one who has thought deeply about the survival of Western civilization. I refer to Sir C. P. Snow, of England. In his brilliant Reed lecture entitled "The Two Cultures and the Scientific Revolution," after expressing his grave concern that the Western democracies were not moving ahead fast enough to meet the challenges of our time—not fast enough to deal with the problem of nuclear warfare and not fast enough to bridge the gap in their alliances and to move forward in the interest of freedom—he said:

> More often than I like, I am saddened by a historical myth. Whether the myth is good history or not, doesn't matter; it is pressing enough for me. I can't help thinking of the Venetian Republic in their last half-century. Like us, they had once been fabulously lucky. They had become rich, as we did, by accident. They had acquired immense political skill, just as we have. A good many of them were tough-minded, realistic, patriotic men. They knew, just as clearly as we know, that the current of history had begun to flow against them. Many of them gave their minds to working out ways to keep going. It would have meant breaking the pattern into which they had crystallized. They were fond of the pattern, just as we—

In the Senate—

> are fond of ours. They never found the will to break it.

Mr. President, may the Senate find the will to break the pattern before it is too late.

I shall not ask for a yea-and-nay vote on the motion before

the Senate to increase the size of the Committee on Finance. The majority leader has indicated that he does not desire a yea and nay vote on either the change that he has proposed in the rule or any of mine. Unless some other Senator forces it, I am not willing to put Senators into what essentially would be an embarrassing position. I know there is no chance of victory.

Mr. President, this is the first Battle of Bull Run. Those of us who wish to modernize the Senate and make it capable of performing its constitutional obligations in a time of great stress, in a time of constant change, and in a time of recurring crises, are going to get licked. But the fight will continue. It will continue until it is won.

The reception in the press and with the public has been far more favorable toward my efforts and those of my colleagues than is the case in the Senate. I shall continue to press, with those who desire to update and streamline the Senate, for the changes of the rules which are now pending in the Committee on Rules and Administration, on which I now have the honor to serve. From time to time we shall bring before the Senate Senate Resolution 9 in order to shock the conscience of the Senate into a realization that it is unethical, wrong, and immoral to deny the right to vote to 56 Senators who desire to change our own rules.

Mr. President, the fight will go on, and one day it will be won. I yield back the remainder of my time.

AMERICAN CENTURY SERIES

Distinguished paperback books in the fields of literature and history.